CW00693680

Life as a
Mother-in-Law

Roles, Challenges, Solutions

Olivia Slaughter, Ph.D.
Jean Kubelun, Ph.D.

Sansevieria
SPRESS

P.O. Box 7196
Thousand Oaks, CA 91359 USA
(818) 889-1856

First published by Dog Ear Publishing
4010 W. 86th Street, Ste H
Indianapolis, IN 46268
www.dogearpublishing.net

ISBN: 978-159858-451-6
LCCN: 2008926706
This book is printed on acid-free paper.

Printed in the United States of America

For Arnie, who always said, "Yes, you can."

For Charles, author himself, who lighted my way and kept me inspired.

*I have not composed this work
to teach people what they do not already know,
but to remind them...
of what is well known to them indeed.
For most of what I say
is nothing more
than what most people do know.*

—Moshe Hayyim Luzzatto
Eighteenth century author of
The Highway of the Upright

Contents

Acknowledgments

 Early on, supporters like Joan Beck, Esther Goldsen, and Christine Wotowiec arranged presentation venues for us in the East, Midwest, and South, and lined up women to attend presentations of the project and to complete our surveys. These women in turn recruited other women, and so the project took on a life of its own, rapidly gathering momentum. Many of these women said "It's about time that this subject got some attention!" and wound up volunteering to help.

Kathryn Jordan has shared her writing expertise throughout the entire book-creating process, and we greatly appreciate her gracious and unflagging support.

Our editor, Catherine Viel, has provided not only invaluable expertise and counsel, but gentle nudging to help us see how we might expand and improve this book. We owe her our deep gratitude.

Technical Web site support and expertise from Keith Galbut, Lindsay Morris, and Michael

Rairden went a long way in making this project possible. It was through their help in developing *www.e-mother-in-law.com* that we were able to communicate with women all over this country and beyond.

We gratefully acknowledge support from our families: Martin and Cynthia Galbut, Mary Rizzoli, Rain Perry, Charles Slaughter, Arnie Kubelun, and Walt and Melinda Kubelun. We are also indebted to loyal cheerleading friends too numerous to mention who kept us moving forward to the finish line.

Prologue

 Mother-in-law challenges are as old as history itself. More than two thousand years ago, the Roman writer Jovenal said, "Domestic accord is impossible as long as the mother-in-law lives."

This book began one summer afternoon several years ago when two old friends were catching up with one another's lives after an interval of several months. Among other topics, the subject of "mother-in-lawing" came up. While both of us have considerable academic and experiential knowledge of the human condition, we discovered that this role of mother-in-law was puzzling and, at times, painful. We knew families with strong in-law bonds, families who were in a perpetual arms race in their relationships, and, of course, everything in between. Like it or not, being a mother-in-law is not voluntary. Live long enough and you will probably be an in-law and may find yourself unprepared for being cast in this role. Happy and pleased as we may be with having a new son- or daughter-in-law, altered behaviors are expected on both sides.

What are these new unwritten rules? And what help is available for the novice as well as the more experienced mother-in-law who needs some guidance from time to time?

From what began with that casual summer afternoon conversation, the subject of mother-in-law relationships grew into an intriguing topic for exploration. As researchers by nature and profession, we naturally turned to books, periodicals, research papers and the Internet to find answers. While there were a fair number of studies that involved other family issues, we were amazed to discover that almost nothing surfaced for mothers-in-law. As might be expected, we found Web sites developed by daughters-in-law in which mothers-in-law were roundly criticized. These sites were generally angry, offensive and demeaning toward mothers-in-law. The information was neither constructive nor insightful. To the best of our knowledge, mothers-in-law don't ride broomsticks, as depicted on one prominent site.

And so we began our journey to research, analyze and synthesize information and then share with others what we learned. Being a mother-in-law can put you in an emotionally vulnerable relationship which has the power to inflict devastating pain as well as uplifting pleasure and fulfillment. Our mission is to provide mothers-in-law with new insights and strategies as well as encouragement to help and inspire.

In our initial surveys of women, we quickly realized we had hit a raw nerve. Almost without exception, the mere mention of a mother-in-law study brought forth instant reactions of interest and "Wait until you hear my story." We even got more than a few "You go, girls!" There was no shortage of volunteers for interviews. It appeared that most women welcomed the opportunity to tell their stories and the connection was instantaneous. Some women needed to talk for hours: it was like a cork popping out of a bottle.

Over the next three years, we initiated several types of surveys to determine the depth and breadth of the problem. A survey of the literature on in-law relationships provided the early foundation for this project. We think the most useful information came from the reported experiences of women like us. We have always believed, even though we are established professionals, that in a great many areas of life, the commonsense wisdom of women can often rival or surpass that of professional experts.

Interviews, both personal and through our Web site survey, made it possible to examine mother-in-law perceptions and experiences. We explored the relationships and patterns of meaning, congruence, conflict and interaction in family life.

All of the personal stories in this book contributed by mothers-in-law are true. We have changed names and other personal information to protect everyone's privacy. Surveys were gathered, many in person and some by telephone, with the largest number being obtained through our Web site. Often the Internet surveys were followed up with telephone interviews.

Our in-depth exploration is based upon the experiences, perspectives and opinions of women representing a wide variety of ages, ethnic groups, geographic locations, religions, education and marital histories. Participants were contacted through civic clubs, professional associations, special interest groups, and various churches, university classes, temples and mosques. Commonalities as well as individual differences were probed with the intention of finding patterns, practices and solutions which might enlighten and support women as they moved into the mother-in-law phase of their lives.

Care was taken to solicit stories about positive, successful relationships as well as those which were troublesome. To give a broader dimension to this study, we also talked with husbands, daughters-in-law and sons-in-law.

For psychological insight, psychologists, psychotherapists, clergy and academics in the field of human relations were also consulted.

Our goals are to fill the gap in mother-in-law relationship knowledge, to support mothers-in-law, and to help us all understand what contributes to familial success and happiness. We are hopeful that this book will provide support and encouragement as well as recognition and reassurance that you are standing on solid ground with most of your mother-in-law peers. We are hopeful, too, that after reading this book you will feel more secure and enlightened, which can lead to better, stronger, wiser, freer, more lighthearted experiences with your adult children, their spouses or partners, and your grandchildren.

We wish to extend heartfelt thanks to each and every woman who generously shared her experience and wisdom to help the rest of us who are struggling to "get it right." We are profoundly grateful.

PART I
Deconstructing the Myth

For many, life as a mother-in-law has never been easy. In Chapters 1 through 4 we explore mother-in-law myths and misconceptions and examine why stereotypes of this important family role can be so damaging. We also describe some pertinent societal changes that occurred over the last several decades and how those changes impact families in general and in-law relationships in particular.

Chapter One
Out of the Mouths of Caves

Everything has been thought of before,
but the problem is to think of it again.
—Johann W. von Goethe

 It all began in the cave. Men went out chasing protein and women were left behind to mind the fire, the children and each other. Hunting was an irregular exercise and often unsuccessful, so women could not always depend on a kill to feed their families and themselves. In fact, male hunting success counted for very little in the daily sustenance of their families. Women foraged for wild berries, honey, tubers and small game to provide most of the calories needed to keep the kinfolk fed. It was the women's foraging that differentially affected and sustained their families' nutritional welfare.

The direct responsibility for the care of the family fell to the women who not only put food on the table, but dealt with the enmeshment of interpersonal relationships of cave life. When men did make a killing, the kill was shared with the girls the hunter was trying to impress or enemies they were working to appease. Therefore, out of expediency, hunting became a political activity as well as a way to survive. One outcome of this way of life was that very little of the meat found its way into the mouths of the hunters' families.

And so, the seeds were sown. Women felt aggressive toward those who came too close and threatened their survival, but were also drawn by a desire for connection with others. The vestiges of this hierarchy, which developed naturally in the ancient caves, are in evidence today. When there is enough of anything to go around—including love and attention—things run smoothly. When there is not enough, jealousy and anger enter the alliances.

Even now, women are often unsettled about other women. This is particularly true when ownership and territory are involved, within families or without. "Women bond with other women, and yet our strongest aggression and our most frightening hostilities may be directed against other women" (Angier, 1999). Surprisingly, relatively few of our aggressive influences are aimed against men because we don't consider men our most serious competitors. Woman to woman competition is much more ingrained in our history.

The strength of female relationships as well as the unease with which we sometimes regard other women are interrelated and can be, in part, attributed to the legacy of dissonance from our ancient cave days. It is a paradox. Women are a potential source of strength—but they can also destroy us. Elizabeth Holland, the English salonist, wrote at the turn of the nineteenth century, "As nobody can do more mischief to a woman than a woman, so perhaps one might reverse the maxim and say nobody can do more good."

Wives, mothers, and mothers-in-law, the purpose of this book is to focus on the good we can do for each other and, by extension, for our families and for the human community as a whole.

Chapter Two
Shedding Stereotypes

There is no such thing as a good stereotype.
Good or bad, it still reduces people to a
consumable, easily digested
prejudged image or word.

—Susan Harjo

 The appellation *mother-in-law* is a prime example of a prejudged image or stereotype. Specific characteristics, like mental cookie cutters, can assign, homogenize, and label all members of groups that deviate from the norm. American journalist Walter Lippman coined the word *stereotype* and defined it as "a picture in our head." He said, "Whether right or wrong, imagination is shaped by the pictures seen. Consequently, these pictures lead to stereotypes that are hard to shake" (Lippman, 1922).

Mother-in-law is just such a stereotype. There exists a universally negative image of her as nagging, meddling, and controlling. There are in-laws other than mothers-in-law who are nagging, meddling, and controlling. Mothers-in-law do not hold a monopoly. It's the behavior, not the specific family role, that needs correction.

Actually, you and most of the people you encounter as you move through life become in-laws, have in-laws and are involved with in-laws one way or another. About half of all women become mothers-in-law, a journey from daughter to daughter-in-law to mother-in-law. This is not an optional journey. Sometimes, instead, it is a forced march. Like it or not, mothers, when your child marries, you become a mother-in-law.

Humor and jokes about one's mother-in-law are a longstanding foundation of comedy. Some television sitcoms have featured stereotypical mothers-in-law (see *Everybody Loves Raymond* and *Married...with Children*). "The humor is based on the idea that the average mother-in-law often considers her son-in-law to be unsuitable for her daughter (or daughter-in-law unsuitable for her son) and usually includes the stereotype that mothers-in-law are generally overbearing, obnoxious, and unattractive" (Wikipedia). Most mother-in-law jokes are translatable to other languages and are easily understandable in most European cultures. Given such wide currency, there are an infinite number of platforms to showcase and perpetuate the stereotype. In this era of political correctness, ethnic groups, the handicapped, and various nationalities are off the table for ridicule. Mothers-in-law remain fair game.

We offer the following negative stereotype examples for those who need a heads-up on the subject. The following "joke" is especially cruel, but representative:

Joe was amazed by the length of the funeral procession going down Main Street. Watching for a while, he observed that the cortege consisted entirely of men and that it was led by a man leading a Doberman pinscher on a leash. When his curiosity got the better of him, he walked up to the man at the front of the line. "Excuse me for interrupting you in your time of grief," said Joe politely, "but I've never seen such a funeral procession. Would you mind telling me who it's for?"

"It's for my mother-in-law," explained the mourner. Tightening the leash, he gestured down at the dog and said, "My Doberman here killed her."

"Gee, that's terrible," commiserated Joe. After a moment he added, "Uh, is there any way you could lend me your dog for a day or so?"

The bereaved son-in-law pointed his thumb over his shoulder and answered, "Get in line."

Another gem, this anagram was found on the Internet. As you probably know, an anagram is a word or phrase created by transposing or rearranging the letters of another word or phrase. "Mother-in-law," when you rearrange the letters, becomes "Woman Hitler."

Then there is Lord Byron, one of the leading figures of the Romantic movement in the early part of the eighteenth century. He was known for his unconventional lifestyle and his marital infidelity (perhaps carrying the Romantic movement too far?). He stated, "I should have blown my brains out, but for the recollection that it would have given pleasure to my mother-in-law."

For sports fans, we paraphrase Kentucky basketball coach Nick Pitino, who labeled his team's defensive alignments "Our mother-in-law set: constant nagging and harassment."

There are many demeaning and exploitative Web sites. One example is www.quisimother.com. When you open the site you are confronted with a picture of a large ape under the title, "MOTHER-IN-LAW MONSTER vs. SILVER-BACKED APE." It features topics such as "Big Balls Mom," "The Blamer," "Sumo Mom," and "Mother-in-Law Jokes" (lots of them), to name just a few. Another Web site, www.insomnomainac.com, is soliciting mother-in-law stories in order to publish a book ridiculing mothers-in-law.

Even the common houseplant with long razor-sharp leaves is called mother-in-law's tongue. It has a botanical name, *sansevieria*, but is most commonly known by the former name. It is also known as snake plant and devil's tongue.

These stories and "jokes" represent a grain of sand on the beach of mother-in-law stories. Mothers-in-law are targets that cross all socio-cultural lines. The gist of most of these jokes, stories, songs, skits, movies and so forth is cruel, one-sided, and dehumanizing. And like all stereotypes, they claim *each* individual human being in a certain group shares a set of common characteristics. Since by definition an individual is different from all other individuals, stereotypes actually are a logical impossibility.

Each of us has a seemingly infinite number of choices about what kind of persona we want to project. Most of us assume a variety of roles: serious at our jobs, sometimes frumpy around the house, loving and supportive with our families, relaxed and uninhibited with our friends, playful with our grandchildren. Behaving differently as our role expectations change is desirable and normal. We can choose not to let the traditional mother-in-law image define us and, instead, be true to ourselves in the adult-to-adult relationships we establish with our grown children. We can each invent a role that works for us. We can disregard how the mother-in-law role is defined by the world of comedy and elsewhere. We are in charge of our own definition.

Chapter Three
Donna Reed Has Left the Building

> *Things do not change, we change.*
> —Henry David Thoreau

 I've been married forty-two years... I've been divorced twice...I'm a widow...I never married... I never worked. I always worked...I have one child...I have ten children...I raised my children during the 50s, 60s, 70s, 80s. I am a grandmother...I have stepchildren and step-grandchildren. I am a nurse, a college professor, a homemaker. I clean houses. I am an employee. I care for my aging parents. I'm peri-menopausal, menopausal, post menopausal... All these voices and more rise to identify who today's women are, where they've been and where they are going. The days of a woman being defined only as a daughter, mother, grandmother or maiden aunt are rapidly disappearing in Western culture.

At the turn of the twentieth century few people lived to see their children, much less their grandchildren, grow to adulthood. Most people were dead at fifty. Today, at fifty, we have another thirty years to live. In the World War II generation, wombs and housewifely skills defined women. Women stayed home and their roles were clearly defined by tradition. Their lives were limited to the domestic arena. They were the kin-keepers, responsible for the happiness and well-being of their family members. They became the family cheerleaders and facilitators.

Along with other family role expectations, their relationships as daughters-in-law were also defined. If they were lucky, the relationship was positive, but regardless, women had the responsibility to keep the peace and ensure domestic tranquility. These "women roles" have very long historical roots, defined by men over hundreds of years and accepted, for the most part without question, generation after generation.

Today, we have a longer, healthier lifespan than at any other time in history. We're having fewer children and spending fewer years raising them. The *Harvard Women's Health Watch* tells us that "63 million women now make up almost half of the U.S. work force, a 56 percent gain since 1950" (*Harvard Women's Health Watch,* "Women, Work, and Stress," September, 2000). "Women increasingly hold professional and managerial jobs, and work in trades previously occupied exclusively by men." In addition, women tend to work full-time or have multiple jobs, and spend more hours than at any other time in history on the job itself. Women also multitask and take on, or must take on, multiple roles such as caregiver for children or elderly relatives, housekeeper or cook, entrepreneur or employee. Perhaps worst of all, it has been found that women's blood pressure and stress hormones stay at increased levels even after they leave their "paid job" for their "unpaid job" at home. Men's stress levels and blood pressure both drop once they punch out from work or other endeavors and head for home. For women, liberation does indeed come with a price!

Add to the above scenario that nearly half of all marriages in the United States today end in divorce, and watch the stress levels rise. The consequence of this phenomenon is that expectations and behaviors change. Parent-child relationships change as well. Many women are pulled outward, away from home and family life. Once they get their lives under control, women are apt to embark on a journey of self-discovery which could lead to further education (formal and informal), volunteer work, travel, and career advances, among other experiences. This period of time, the "rest" of our lives, which is lived for the self rather than for others, can leave women with far less time and energy to devote to parenting and in-law activities. Life now has to be triaged.

A *New York Times* article entitled "Why America Judges Amy's Mother," by Margaret Guilette, suggested that the macro changes in our culture affect mother-in-law relationships (*New York Times,* April 2, 2000). Phrases such as *empty nest syndrome* and *Oedipal failure to detach* creep into our vocabulary. Mothers-in-law are said to hover, to be bossy, to be over-invested and/or interfering. *Matrophobia*, a cultural disease acquired by adult children, preaches that mothers and mothers-in-law need not be treated with consideration and respect. They can be viewed as Eveready plug-ins who stand ready to fulfill their children's psychological needs, but only upon request. In an era of heightened youth cultism, and the "me first" ideation of newer generations, parents—mothers and mothers-in-law in particular—are required to back off and renegotiate on terms the children set. Many times "children" are not aware of and will not detect their mother's loss of self when time lost to her needs is time gained for theirs. Danish philosopher Soren Kierkegaard expressed the problem this way: "The greatest danger, that of losing one's own self, may pass off quietly as if it were nothing: every [other] loss, that of an arm, a leg, five dollars…is sure to be noticed."

Another new cultural term, *post-maternal*, is used to describe mothers of grown children.

Post-maternal women are often exposed to harsh, disrespectful attitudes and even contempt. In a 2000 issue of *Modern Maturity*, in an article entitled "How Not to be a Monster-in-Law," mothers-in-law were patronized as "buttinskies" and chided that "there is more than one way to make potato salad." Really!

What does all this mean to us in the context of being a mother-in-law? With these profound life changes and new expectations, family strains can leak out in many directions, including interpersonal relationships. As women modify their own life roles, many make the transition from basking in the reflected glory of their families to seeking and finding their own place in the sun. The traditional mother-role has been partially, if not completely, reframed. Women moved into the world, found work and achieved successes of their own, and at the same time, they continued their domestic roles. This major shift away from the home and into the world, while simultaneously experiencing their children's new roles, can be a major source of friction between generations of women. Tensions may arise around such simple issues as who does the cooking, cleaning and even child care. Some older women may find it hard to understand that their daughters-in-law don't iron, do laundry or clean the house. Younger women may not understand the history, customs and culture that kept their mothers and mothers-in-law functioning as *house wives*. The rejection of a mother-in-law's values and lifestyle can often be interpreted as a rejection of the person herself.

Our membership in this sisterhood of women, for better or worse, is in the twenty-first century. We need not be constrained by outmoded ways of thinking, acting, even feeling. We *can* be active, vital, actualized human beings who balance work and family and play and strive for fulfillment on all levels. We *can* renew and recharge ourselves in a way previous generations never dreamed of doing. We *can* focus on the only life we can control, which is our own, and we *can* make choices to put positive energy into ourselves and not into emotions that are destructive or counterproductive.

We can do all this because we do not live in an earlier time when roles were circumscribed and autonomy was not available to women. Do any of us wish for those simpler, "easier" times to return? There's no contest, really. At least not for us or for most of the women who shared their stories of struggle and quiet triumph for this book.

Chapter Four
The Family Prism

In each of us there is a little of all of us.
—Georg Christoph Lichtenberg

 Families today take many forms: one parent, two parents, foster parents, grandparents...even great-grandparents are raising children. Aunts and uncles and/or stepparents move in, move out or stay for the duration. Families may include parents as well as children who are gay or lesbian. A family can be as small as two adults sharing a home, or as large as several adults and a dozen children, with three and four generations living together more or less harmoniously.

The 2000 U.S. Census Report tells us there are increasingly complex family relationships as compared to previous generations:

1. There is a thirty-year trend away from married-with-children. This reflects social changes that began in the 1970s.

2. In 2000, there were fewer than one in four homes that included people who were married with children.

3. In 2000, single-mother homes had increased by 25 percent.

4. In 2000, single-father homes had increased by 62 percent. Over the years the courts have become friendlier to fathers seeking custody.

5. In 2000, unmarried-partner households had increased by 72 percent. The largest gains in this sector occurred in the Bible Belt and across the Great Plains.

There are many factors that contributed to these changes. Robert T. Michael, in his address at an Emory University conference, suggested that there are three key changes within the economy that affected family roles. First, higher wages for all workers encouraged more women to enter the workplace. Second, the U.S. economy shifted to jobs that were not physically demanding, thus equalizing labor requirements for male and female workers; more married women entered the workplace, transforming the family. And third, government expanded its role in education and social security, subsidizing higher education. "As the young people gain higher education skills, and the care of preschool children becomes the responsibility of schools or the government, the role of the family in these tasks declines" (Michael, 2003). These factors, among others, shifted the more traditional marriage patterns. Also, as women were more and more able to earn their own way in the world, divorce became more affordable since there was no longer one spouse with no marketable skills. The advent of effective, reliable birth control is another factor in the changing social roles. Women were free to pursue higher education, travel the world, and make a commitment to a career without fear of pregnancy.

It is clear that the American family is being redefined. This glacial-like reshaping foretells role and expectation changes for in-law relationships, too. In previous generations, mothers-in-law were a part of the extended family. Often, they played a role in rearing their grandchildren. Families tended to stay in one community for generations, sometimes sharing houses, sometimes living within a small, circumscribed community. Now, small families move across town, across the country, wherever careers or corporations demand. This fluidity impacts traditional family expectations and relationships.

Government policies have also changed. For example, there are accommodations for live-in relationships, and those changes have been institutionalized in both language and law. With all of these social forces, differences in values, lifestyles, child rearing practices and other variables could easily lead to clashes among nuclear as well as extended family members. The changes from more traditional to non-traditional families will impact almost all of us.

And so it follows that the role of the mother-in-law is shrinking along with the diminishing traditional family patterns. When a child marries, will all members of the combined new families bond together and live happily ever after? This is a widely accepted myth perpetuated by young brides and grooms. It is part of the fantasy world they experience as lovers and newlyweds. In many cases, this does not happen. Perhaps affianced and newlywed couples are victimized by the "fantasy," or perhaps they want desperately to believe in a big happy extended family post-wedding.

However, the reality is that getting married brings together two previously unrelated groups, and requires family members to establish close links with others they have no part in selecting and might, given a choice, prefer to have no association with whatsoever.

Families, even nuclear families with love and rapport in abundance, have disagreements, dislikes, and disappointments among themselves. Why then would we expect in-laws to smoothly blend into some storied fairy tale?

Communicating with in-laws often presents a range of challenges for the newly created families. In-laws may have different conversational styles and/or speech habits. They may be talkative or very quiet, they may be direct or indirect, they may speak loudly or softly. There will surely be differences of taste, experience, and world views to say nothing of differences in education, religion, culture, and socioeconomic status. Political differences may require careful eggshell walking. Each in-law interaction becomes a prism through which the words and behaviors of the now expanded family members are refracted. The challenge is to realign past family patterns and create new, more inclusive ones. Actually, many families may conclude that these new patterns refresh and enrich their lives by introducing new interests, personalities, and points of view, not to mention cuisine.

Richard Carlson, in his book, *How to Be Happy No Matter What*, suggests the principal of separate realities may be operating here. This principal states, "The differences among individuals are every bit as vast as those among different cultures…it is not a matter of tolerating differences in behavior but of understanding that it literally can't be any other way" (Carlson, 1997). Each individual person—mother, father, bride, groom—brings a unique set of understandings, experiences and expectations into the mix.

Peering through the family prism, then, reminds us of the absolute need as individuals to remain open, flexible, and tolerant of human differences. They bring gifts as well as challenges.

PART II
What Sets Us Apart
The Top Five Causes of In-Law Problems

*In Part II we will discuss a variety of in-law
challenges, beginning with the five most
troublesome aspects of in-law relationships,
and concluding with a second set of relevant
but somewhat lesser issues.*

Chapter Five
Finding Your Balance

Happiness is equilibrium.
Shift your weight. Equilibrium is pragmatic.
You have to get everything into proportion.
You compensate, rebalance yourself so that
you maintain your angle to the world.
When the world shifts, you shift.

—Tom Stoppard

 Imagine a mobile representing your family relationships. This creative and communicative metaphor visualizing the interrelatedness of family relationships is suggested by Sharon Wegscheider in her book, *Another Chance* (1981). With a nod to Virginia Satir, who originated the concept, Wegscheider invites us to envision a mobile as an analogy for family. "Let us say you have a mobile with five or six beautiful butterflies, all of different sizes, suspended by strings from three sticks. The butterflies represent the family members and sticks are the family roles. The whole thing has been designed to keep its equilibrium. If a puff of wind hits it, it responds immediately by rocking and twisting. This is the beauty of a mobile, ever moving yet ever returning to equilibrium."

Taking this analogy further, if two mobiles, representing a husband and wife and their respective families, are combined into one, each element or butterfly needs to find a new space and a new balance. The sticks and strings will need to be readjusted to accommodate the larger, more inclusive set of butterflies. The challenge becomes how to realign past patterns and create new, expanded but balanced patterns—and there is no manual or road map to help with the process.

Traditionally, mothers take a central place in each family mobile. They orchestrate the contacts and relationships among everyone in the kin network. They make the social connections, secure times and places for family events and, in general, keep kin communications going. It makes sense, then, that the most ambivalent of all family relationships is between mothers-in-law and daughters-in-law. There can only be one person in this central role, so one of them must give way to the other. It is the natural order of things that the daughter-in-law will ascend and mothers and mothers-in-law will play supporting roles. This is as it should be; however, mothers-in-law should not now be considered yesterday's news.

Just as the mother's key role in the family mobile is going to shift and somewhat diminish after the wedding, so will the mother-in-law's role shift and change. The tension between a mother-in-law who has been displaced and a daughter-in-law who has moved to a more prominent family position is almost inevitable. These two women have no bedrock of shared experience to draw upon, so sharing turf can become adversarial. Sons-in-law, on the other hand, have a much lower profile in this respect, as do other in-law relationships. There are fewer competition issues; the stakes are not nearly as high.

Naturally, it isn't uncommon for all in-laws to have difficult periods, which create periodic family mobile turbulence. Personality traits, expectations, a shifting of power, and generational conflicts all bubble to the surface and require adjustments and, hopefully, resolution. Women in our culture are basically left alone in most families to establish a new role as best they can. We are all imperfect human beings so it easy to see how difficult this re-balancing can be. People and circumstances change over time; in-law relationships are always a work in progress. The challenge is to stay connected through the ups and downs, and, if possible, balance the mobile once more.

For some families, however, comfortable equilibrium is never achieved, and the mobile remains permanently out of balance.

When Janna's daughter married a man who was not "my kind of people," Janna was devastated. As the couple was driving away after the wedding, this traditional and elegant Southern woman thought in disbelief, "There's this man taking away my daughter!" Janna described her son-in-law as a "rough and tumble" truck driver who "hadn't finished growing up." This man married her daughter, a professional in the medical field. There were significant social, economic, and educational differences between the two.

Over the years, Janna largely refrained from being openly critical of her son-in-law's "financial irresponsibility" which caused her daughter to work longer hours and sometimes two jobs. The couple did, however, produce two successful, well-adjusted, and loving sons, one of whom in particular was very close to Janna. On a visit to his grandmother (and over a couple of drinks), Janna tried to "set the record straight about why I didn't want my daughter to marry your father."

After thirty years, Janna hadn't let go of her disappointment. The result of this incident was that she lost some of her beloved grandson's respect, and the relationship was never quite the same again. While Janna might have behaved differently without the inhibition-reducing effects of alcohol, it was almost inevitable that this conversation, or one like it, would at some point occur, with similar, devastating results.

Janna, by not letting go of her long-held frustration and disapproval, overlooked two very important facts: first, her daughter and son-in-law have a successful thirty-year marriage; and next, there are two well-adjusted, successful grandsons who are products of this marriage. Sad to say, Janna was blinded to what's ultimately important: the success of her daughter's marriage. Income, education, and social discrepancies were compensated for by other values, doubtless including the fact the couple loved one another. In Janna's generation and social context, this match may have been considered unsuitable and would probably have been prevented by the bride's family.

The generation gap is many times a hard bridge to cross and sometimes requires repeated attempts to succeed. Some never make it. Holding on to such disapproving and negative feelings, as Janna did, is a trait shared by a number of other women in our survey. Clinging to these feelings, regardless of the reason, is self-destructive and counterproductive. Even though it may be difficult, it is simply time to let these feelings go. Instead of harboring disappointment and frustration, commit to forgiving, forgetting and moving on.

An important and frequently recurring theme of this book is that letting go of negativity empowers your life. When you take control, you stop allowing an unhappy situation to control you. You may say, "Easier said than done." We say, "You'd be surprised how much less difficult life is when you make up your mind to let go of the albatross you've been carrying and move on." When the weight of negative feelings is dispersed, you'll feel lighter and more at peace.

Over the long term, forgiveness and the resolution of your in-law problems may require far less energy than wasting precious years feeling continually frustrated. You will be rewarded with a richer, more honest and more fulfilling life. And just maybe when you have achieved this balance, the troubling family relationships will take on a different perspective.

Frieda suffers from a problem similar to Janna's although the situation is quite different. Her son, an only child, was raised as an Episcopalian. He married a Jewish woman fifteen years his senior. After the marriage he converted to Judaism and had a bar mitzvah. Both are scientists with strong ties to Israel and divide their time between the two countries. On the rare occasions that Frieda has been invited by her son to special family events which include his wife, Frieda's grandson, and the wife's family, the languages have been Hebrew and French. Frieda speaks neither and feels like an outsider. She is bitter and complains, "I'm rejected so I reject, too." She is resigned to her life without family contact. Frieda tries not to dwell upon her grief but admits that sometimes she does feel anger and hurt at what she perceives as abandonment by her son. Having no contact with her daughter-in-law and no relationship with her grandson adds to the hurt.

This is a painful story for anyone to read. Frieda is enmeshed in her anger and resentment in spite of her efforts to minimize or deny them. This serves to exacerbate those feelings and blocks efforts to find some approach which could put her in charge of finding a path to improve the situation. Instead of assuming the role of a victim, Frieda has the option of taking a proactive position. Regular communication with her family via e-mail or personal notes might be a good place to start; sharing something of her life such as photographs, holiday and birthday cards or small gifts, if appropriate, could also help. Frieda might go further and take a class in conversational French or Hebrew. It is entirely likely that the initiation of effort on her part would pay positive dividends.

Sometimes the desire to interfere with a child's marriage is almost overpowering, but circumspection may be a wiser, though more difficult, choice.

Noelle, a retired legal secretary, and her husband made the difficult decision to hold back until their daughter was ready to reach out to them. Noelle's daughter, a very attractive young respiratory therapist, was swept off her feet by a man thirteen years her senior. This man was a heart surgeon and professor at the teaching hospital where the young woman worked. He was wealthy and highly educated, but also a heavy drinker. During a weekend they spent in Las Vegas the marriage took place on a bet.

Following this impromptu wedding, the doctor wanted nothing to do with his new wife's family, whom he considered to be inferior in every way. The doctor insisted that the two families had nothing in common other than his spouse, and refused to have anything to do with them. The daughter became estranged from her own family and was not able to reconnect until the marriage was over some two years later.

During the marriage, Noelle and her husband watched from a distance as their daughter was swept up in a world that she was unprepared to live in. Her new life included luxury she had never before experienced but also life in the fast lane, which unfortunately included another new element: substance abuse. Noelle and her husband worried and felt the pressure of wanting to rescue her but didn't believe that would really be the best thing for their daughter in the long run.

Sure enough, in two years the marriage crashed. They felt that until their daughter appealed to them for help they'd have to stand patiently by and hope the damage could be remedied in time. It took many months for the daughter to recover (and the parents as well).

It is very difficult for parents to stand by when they see their adult children involved with substance abuse or suffering any kind of abuse at the hand of another. The challenge is knowing when to cross the line and step in. In Noelle's case it was clear that she and her husband had to wait until their daughter finished living out her fantasy life and asked for support. In other cases, great pressure is felt when trying to determine whether or not to step in and seek action. If you find yourself faced with this type of situation, make sure it is a CRITICAL issue and always consider possible outcomes before you decide to intervene.

Personal ethics are another dimension where balance turbulence may be experienced. The story of Marcy is a case in point.

Marcy's son married a glamorous woman who, Marcy discovered, would regularly buy expensive clothes, wear them to an affair, and then return the outfit for a refund the following day. Marcy was conflicted about reporting this to her son, who was blissfully unaware of this particular eccentricity in his wife. She felt she might be "tattling" so she resisted the inner pressure to speak up. To add to this dilemma, the daughter-in-law was following a pattern set down by her mother and grandmother, making it very awkward for Marcy to confront her directly.

Later, however, when it became known that her daughter-in-law was scamming doctors by keeping medical appointments and then not paying and simply moving on to other doctors, Marcy did speak with her son. As a medical professional, Marcy knew that for her, this behavior was simply beyond the pale. Not long afterward, the son's "bliss" went south as his infatuation with his bride hit the rocks of reality. The couple divorced shortly thereafter.

Some mothers-in-law have learned to maintain balance successfully by blending unfamiliar customs and values through trial and error, others through hard-won experience or by some unique intuition or stroke of luck. The stories below exemplify the positive outcomes achieved by resourceful, intelligent, and creative women who were faced with challenging in-law situations.

Margot shared that her daughter-in-law came from a mostly uneducated family and "is not trying to learn." However, this daughter-in-law makes her son happy and has produced three healthy, happy boys. While she wishes her son had chosen differently, Margot wisely recognizes that her son's and grandsons' happiness is the most important blessing she has. And while lack of formal education can be a drawback, people often possess valuable non-traditional wisdom, skills, and a commonsense intelligence which should not be overlooked or undervalued.

Hana is a good example of overcoming a potential culture clash with grace and integrity.

Originally from Egypt, Hana now lives in Michigan. She explained that in her culture the expectation is the daughter-in-law will live with her husband's family, which in Hana's case was for twenty long years. Her mother-in-law made all the decisions, including issues of family finances, discipline of Hana's children, what to serve for dinner each night and even on which wall to hang a picture. However, Hana believes that a newlywed woman, by nature, wants to run her home according to her own wishes. This young woman would come from a different home, have her own tastes and values, and would want to raise her children the way her own mother brought her up.

Hana described two types of Egyptian mothers-in-law: those who have suffered through the traditional experience, like Hana, and want to break the cycle of dominance, and those who say, "I suffered and now it is your turn to suffer as I did." Hana, who now lives with her son and daughter-in-law in Michigan, has chosen the former way and has handed over the running of her home to her daughter-in-law. "You will be the master," she says. She concludes by telling us, "It is very hard to withdraw but you must. Otherwise you are interfering with the freedom which they must have." Hana has chosen a healthy balance.

Other cultural differences can become problematic around holiday and family traditions.

Jean is an office manager whose daughter, an only child, married an Englishman. When their child's first Christmas arrived, the grandparents came from England. Their tradition was one gift per person each Christmas. Jean's tradition was to fill up the car with family gifts and celebrate with wild abandon. This prospect presented a dilemma with potential for damaging the holiday and the relationships. Jean, her daughter and son-in-law hit upon a plan to have two celebrations, one on Christmas Eve with lots of gifts and without the son-in-law's parents, and another on Christmas Day, when the celebration was English-style with one gift each. Differences in celebrating the festivities were resolved to everyone's satisfaction; both traditions were respected and honored. Once again, balance was achieved.

~ ~ ~

Joannie is a step mother-in-law who reports that she never had problems with her stepsons. However, when one of them became engaged to a woman who was a marketing specialist for a very prestigious antiques auction house, the family became embroiled in turmoil for the entire nine-month engagement. The bride-to-be, an only child of middle-class parents, had been coddled and pampered her whole life as if she were a princess. She seemed riveted to symbols of wealth, status and luxury. Elaborate fairytale wedding plans were hatched with no thought to cost. Furthermore, the bride-to-be was prone to judge others by their clothing, jewelry, cars and homes. Even though her stepson and the family had no financial concerns connected to the cost of the wedding, the planning intruded on their personal lives and time. No one seemed to want to refuse the future bride anything, and she would not have taken "no" for an answer anyway.

Finally, Joannie put her foot down. She told Bridezilla, "Look, we are put on this earth together. I can learn from you and you can learn from me." It seemed that establishing boundaries and imposing limits were new experiences for her future daughter-in-law, but once she adjusted, the young woman became more accepting of what she would have rejected earlier as criticism or simply ignored.

A new, more balanced relationship between the two future in-laws ensued. Now, Joannie observes that her daughter-in-law can still be quite self-indulgent at times; everyone takes it lightly and the family gently chides her when she "goes over the top." A new baby is expected before long, and challenges are arising again. A prince or princess will be entering Joannie's world, you see, and now the family is able to deal with the "royal" issues in a more loving and effective way.

It is important to recognize that Joannie was able to talk with her future daughter-in-law firmly and honestly without putting her down or disparaging her in any way. The same holds true for "gentle chiding." Some words of caution: if you choose to use gentle chiding, tread lightly and do it only after you have established a foundation of love and trust. If the foundation isn't established, the chiding may be interpreted as criticism and backfire.

Miriam, who is Jewish, has one child, a son who married into a Polish Catholic family. Almost everything changed for him: religion, holidays and celebrations, consumer habits, and even cuisine. And, of course, everything changed for Miriam, as well. She commented that while her son's new relationships were worrisome in some ways, in other ways the changes have been rewarding because the family has been extended and has opened up new enjoyable experiences. When Miriam was widowed, her daughter-in-law's family were very kind, loving, and supportive. They include her in family celebrations and the holidays are festive. Miriam comments, "Coming from a small family, I am especially appreciative of that." Her balance is restored.

~ ~ ~

Finally, there is Kristin, whose son married outside the family ethnic group. Other than this difference, all other qualities were compatible, including educational background, social and economic status, religious affiliation, age, and interests. In this case, Kristin's husband did not approve of the match while Kristin was very positive about her new daughter-in-law. All other family members agreed with her, feeling that all the background similarities outweighed the ethnic difference.

As time passed, the father-in-law mellowed. Now that he is a grandfather, it is a non-issue since the new butterfly took his place on the mobile. Kristin does not believe in interfering in the lives and choices of her children because "each is responsible for their own lives and have their own way of seeing the world."

Achieving balance is our message. Whether it is your own or encouraging it on the family mobile, achieving balance is the healthiest, happiest, most productive way to build your life. We are all different, and so being able to appreciate others has to be part of our mission. In those instances when despite all your efforts to make a difficult relationship work you still can't find balance, it is probably best to distance yourself. Maybe not forever but until you feel safe in trying again.

Regardless, take care of yourself first. Balance is, first and foremost, an inside job.

Chapter Six
Under New Management

Woman's two great tasks are to shape her unity with the child in a harmonious manner and later to dissolve harmoniously.

—Deutsch

 In our culture, mothers of growing or grown children often find themselves caught in a web of contradictions. We are expected to be intensely involved with our babies, measuring food, behavior and developmental milestones to make sure our children have the best we can give them. As our children grow up and away, we are expected to put aside our mothering instincts and step back, letting our children go on about their lives without our participation or input. It can seem as though we have lost our purpose and value. "When for years mothers have been emotionally invested in the well-being of their families and physically responsive to their needs, they don't easily change that behavior or turn off emotion like a light switch" (Jarvis, 2001).

The challenge then becomes how to realign our past family patterns to create new and exciting paths. Revising our lives begins with letting go of the marriage that was defined by the children and creating in its place a new one in which the partners are once again concentrating on each other. For couples, that could mean expanding interests together, as well as finding new interests to bring back into the marriage. For single-parent families, it is also a time to spread your wings and see what the world contains after the children leave.

The need to renew your marriage or forge a new identity other than that of parent can be exciting, stimulating, and freeing. However, it can also be unsettling and sad. Couples may draw apart; single parents may weep and/or fall into a depression. It is essential to remember that the changes in family life are inevitable. Your children should and will leave, just as you, yourself, once did. Eric Erikson describes this state of life as "generativity vs. stagnation" (Erikson, 1959). There is more to life than children. Now is the time to open up for new things, to give back some of your experiences to others, to generate rather than stagnate.

Sometimes mothers are hardly aware of how much their self-identity has been modified over the years while their children were growing up. Holding onto family ties too tightly is counterproductive and puts family relationships at great risk. The idea is to hold, but with an open hand, allowing mothers to let go and thereby facilitate their child's transition to independence, marriage or an adult partnership.

Of course, a child's transition to independence often brings new daughters- or sons-in-law into the picture. Sometimes, as the following stories show, our children-in-law present unusually difficult challenges after the wedding.

Margaret has a controlling daughter-in-law who came right out and said that her husband was under new management…and that he must choose between his mother and her. "He can't have both of us: he can only have one." In this family, the daughter-in-law has issued a set of child-visit rules that her mother-in-law must follow even in her own home. These rules include: do not give hugs without permission, do not pick the children up to hug them, and worst of all, do not give them anything to eat at Margaret's own house.

Margaret expressed her dilemma this way: "Currently, I have a seven-year-old granddaughter who refuses to eat or drink anything but water at my home because she gets in trouble when she returns home and has to give an account of what she has consumed while here." Margaret said that her daughter-in-law "has a lot of insecurity and issues from her own childhood that bleed into today and, unfortunately, have affected our relationship in a negative way."

Daughters-in-law with damaged self-esteem can wreak havoc on families. Consider the impact of this story upon Margaret, who feels rejected, resentful and powerless. Consider the emotional impact on the children who are being taught to reject physical affection from their grandparents, and the stress on their father who is being torn in two directions. Consider also that there is a long tradition of grandparents who occasionally "spoil" grandchildren with treats that are not often or may never be available at home. Margaret has been denied this pleasure, and so have the grandchildren.

Obviously, there is much work to be done in this extended family. Most reasonable people would consider the daughter-in-law's visitation rules excessive or even destructive. First—at the very least, because the children are being "victimized"—the grandparents, their son, and the daughter-in-law need to restructure expectations for grandparent/grandchildren visits. This would ideally include abolishing or altering the punitive "rules" that are distressing to both generations. Second, if those rules are *not* relaxed, it must be acknowledged that there is a real possibility that the children will begin to emulate their mother and develop hostile, controlling behaviors themselves. And third, for her own sake, the daughter-in-law needs to be encouraged to consider seeking help in dealing with her control issues.

One positive aspect of this situation can be built upon: there continues to be contact between the families. The grandchildren are allowed to visit, so the relationships have not completely broken down. Another positive aspect of this situation is Margaret's ability to have compassion for her daughter-in-law's past experiences.

Margaret will need to continue her relationship with her grandchildren in whatever way she can. Children do grow up, and the good memories of their grandparents are forever embedded in their thoughts and feelings. At least the grandchildren will have that.

~ ~ ~

In Susan's case, she believes her daughter-in-law uses her grandson as a control to keep Susan and her husband "in line." If they do anything her daughter-in-law doesn't like, she will not allow them to spend any time with their grandson. This is rather noticeable as they all attend the same church where her daughter-in-law makes a great show of not letting them spend any time at church with the baby (much less at home).

~ ~ ~

Lynn tells us, "My daughter-in-law is a controller, very manipulative, and keeps my grandchildren from me." They live five minutes away. Lynn said that her daughter-in-law told her son that if he doesn't do as she says, she'll leave and take the children with her. Lynn's son complies.

Grandchildren can be the leverage used by daughters-in-law to gain control. And it is difficult, indeed, near impossible and unnatural for grandmothers to relinquish precious time with their grandchildren. There are no easy solutions for this painful state of affairs. However, giving all the power to a daughter-in-law who holds grandchildren hostage is no solution, either: by giving up all control to a daughter-in-law, the mother-in-law loses part of herself as well. This may work for a while, but then the price becomes too high. At some point, it is important for us, as mothers-in-law, to reclaim our lives even if it means giving up the idea of a perfect fantasy relationship with our children and grandchildren.

Consider the following stories from mothers-in-law who have found a way to live with this challenge.

Joan has a daughter-in-law who "has broken our family up. She will not allow my son to talk to or see anyone in our family." Joan says she's had to learn that some people can't accept what a loving and welcoming person she is.

There is a serious stand-off here. It seems to have started with the birth of the grandson. The daughter-in-law just wanted everything to be HER family. Joan's son is in the military, and without him participating in finding some resolution and peace, there seems to be little hope that this problem will get resolved.

Joan concluded that, "Spending more time with family and friends is what gets me through this phase my son calls 'marriage.'"

~ ~ ~

Kate describes a manipulative daughter-in-law who ignores and rejects her husband's immediate and extended family. The daughter-in-law refuses to allow her grandson to spend time with "the other side of the family" yet stays in close touch with her own mother, who lives four hundred miles away, speaking with her several times each day by phone.

In addition, the daughter-in-law sends mixed messages, causing more confusion for Kate. "Yo-yo" is Kate's summary of the relationship with her daughter-in-law. "One week the relationship can be as natural as that of a mother/daughter and the next week we are totally out of the picture as if we didn't exist." Kate has given up working to understand her daughter-in-law's behavior and concludes: "I'm just learning I have to live my own life. My husband and I now have the freedom to do whatever we want to do without having to consult four totally different family members' schedules. If we want to go out of town, we no longer have to make child care arrangements or plan for activities we don't enjoy. We please ourselves. Next Christmas we want to be away from all the pain and stress, so we're going on a cruise."

~ ~ ~

Molly had to let go of a close relationship with her daughter because of many problems with the son-in-law. Molly and her husband opted to move seventeen hundred miles away and "built our dream house and got a dog to substitute for the void. While it hurts emotionally to be away from our daughter, we are healthier and happier here."

~ ~ ~

Evelyn has a similar story. She "put up with" her daughter-in-law's controlling behavior for years, just so she could remain close to her son and her grandchildren. When her son needed money to start his dental practice, Evelyn and her husband dipped into their retirement funds to help him. After several years of discord, there was a huge blow-up and Evelyn's daughter-in-law gave her husband an ultimatum: *Either they go, or I do*. There was no contact between the two families at all. The daughter-in-law would not relent and Evelyn and her husband were denied any contact with their grandchildren. After three years of this, Evelyn and her husband sold their house and moved to California just to get away from the pain.

These solutions may appear a little extreme, but we suspect they are more common than we know. Finding and enjoying a life without children and grandchildren being central to your whole self is the beginning of a new phase in your life. This new stage can be exciting and freeing. And, out of this new life may come a new understanding and resolution of old problems. Once separate lives and interests are established, old resentments and hostilities may take on less importance and begin to fade. New perspectives can lead to resolutions over time, once each party has some breathing room.

Some mothers-in-law in our research offer their advice, gained from hard-won experience.

Cassie decided to "let go" in order to keep peace in the family. Cassie has difficulty with one daughter-in-law out of three. "This daughter-in-law seems to resent my hugging my son or showing that I love him." She believes this boils down to jealousy…two women loving the same person. She recalls, "There is a verse in the Bible that says, 'Get along with others as much as you are able.'" And that's what Cassie tries to do. "We can't control everything others say and do. We can only be responsible for our own words and actions."

Christine, a retired administrator and an enlightened mother-in-law, offers this advice:

"Have your children and your in-law children be a part of your life but not the focus of your life. They have to have their lives; you need to have your own life. A life that's satisfying so you don't need to depend on your children for your satisfactions and you're so involved in their lives you feel you have a right to give advice. You really don't unless asked, and even when asked, you have to be very careful of the kinds of advice you offer. Certainly, unless there's an abusive situation or something that's very serious, they have to work out their good times and their bad times together.

"And so you have to work at your relationships with them just as you do with your friends. You don't criticize your friends or they are probably not your friends. And if you want a positive relationship, you need to be a friend. Be undemanding. Don't expect them to make your life, either...Don't obligate them. It's hard to draw a line between being generous and crossing the line into where you make them feel guilty...The things you give them can become a burden...Bottom line: Have a life of your own, enjoy your life, and let them live their lives."

~ ~ ~

Johanna, artist/journalist, believes that:

"The mother-in-law relationship has the potential to be truly onerous, truly wonderful, or somewhere in between. It's all about expectations." Johanna has been fortunate with her own in-law relationships, including with her own mother- and father-in-law. However, others within her close family have less happy situations.

In many cases described in this chapter, the daughter-in-law has taken management or ex-ecutive privilege to the level of dictatorship. This behavior can come from feeling powerless or in-secure and/or having a lack of trust in self and others. From these and other feelings comes a need to win issues by forcing others into submis-sion. We do note that none of the mothers-in-law in these stories questioned the absence of their own child's involvement. The responsibility, in each case, was laid at the foot of the in-law child.

And therein lies part of the problem. If at all possible, mothers need to step in and refuse to accept less than honesty and respect from the new management team—both their own child and the child's spouse. There are many ways to approach this. All situations are different, but we recommend you start by reading, developing, and practicing the statements in Appendix B, "I" Messages.

Most of the heartfelt stories in this chapter illuminate this truth: there are no simple solutions. Each of us wants the unconditional love of our families, including our in-law relatives, although many of us will (and must) settle for less. We have found, over the years, that keeping things in perspective and developing and maintaining a good sense of humor will go a long way toward attaining a healthy outlook for ourselves and the families we love.

Chapter Seven
The *Bite Your Tongue* Club

Be not too tame, neither, but let your own
discretion be your tutor; suit the action to
the word, the word to the action.

—William Shakespeare

 Of all the responses to our survey, the one that engendered the most reaction was the "bite your tongue" advice. The responses ran the gamut from never, ever saying anything, to saying whatever you want whenever you want. However, a virtual avalanche of responses expressed belief that the best course of action to preserve peace in the extended family was to "keep your mouth shut."

Many women did not feel free to express their opinion or offer advice or make a suggestion for fear of being misunderstood and/or rejected. When pressed, some women could recount personal horror stories about what happened when they chose *not* to bite their tongues. Obviously, the solutions to this very worrisome challenge do not come from either extreme. Saying anything and everything to your in-laws is a recipe for disaster. Likewise, keeping everything bottled up inside is a surefire way to invite trouble, including well-documented physical and emotional distress that can be brought on by suppressing your feelings.

We believe it is time to explore the age-old adage that a mother-in-law should essentially be seen and not heard. Does this adage mean we should let little misunderstandings grow into a war? Should we stand on the sidelines, humbly waiting for permission to speak, permission to be ourselves? How did the rules of communication change once we became a mother-in-law? In years past, young adults turned to their parents and parents-in-law for advice; grandparents were involved with their grandchildren. Now, many times there is a frozen, polite tolerance for the elder members of any family group, or even worse, downright disrespect.

We certainly do not advocate a tell-all, interfering, critical, judgmental approach to your grown children—married or unmarried. Rather, we suggest a middle ground where ideas and feelings can be expressed and there is mutual respect. We believe this is a comfortable, healthy way to live.

One mother-in-law in particular expressed it this way.

Luna, a professor and psychologist, says, "Holding my tongue when I disagree with any of my three sons and their wives, allowing them to set their pace and distance [is difficult]. I am usually intimate with friends quickly and [I] struggle with the fact that the role and all its preconceived notions in people's minds prevents that from happening [with my children]." Luna goes on to say, "I am glad you are doing this [book]. The societal mind-set is a trap and must change."

There were a fair number of women who said, with great sincerity, to always bite your tongue.

Sharon, an office worker, stated that the best way to preserve peace in the family is to "keep your mouth shut, keep your mouth shut, keep your mouth shut."

~ ~ ~

Elise, from England, recommended: "Make sure that anything you say or do could not be construed as criticism or interference. Be careful about not offering advice and NEVER criticize the grandchildren."

~ ~ ~

Schenken, schveigen, schivngen is a German mother-in-law saying that Kate, a translator, shares with us. It means "Swallow [your hurt], keep quiet, and give great gifts." Kate's challenge, like so many others in this study, is "Keeping my mouth shut and keeping my thoughts to myself."

~ ~ ~

Mary, a hairdresser, works on keeping her opinions to herself. She said, "I'm a doer and want to help out and sometimes need to sit back."

It is clear that these women, and others, were willing to keep their ideas, suggestions and thoughts bottled up in order to maintain a semblance of family harmony. While this goal is admirable, it is achieved only when the mothers-in-law are willing to sacrifice a part of themselves.

Most women work hard to avoid offending their grown children and spouses. They struggle to maintain a relationship, even in the face of insults and rejection. Obviously, the choice is a personal one and depends upon the individual personalities of the people involved. At times it must feel like the legendary Procrustes who offered travelers a pitiless bed. If they were too tall, he cut off their feet so the bed could accommodate them. If they were too short, he stretched them. No matter how we work to fit our relationships into convenient molds, short of cutting off parts of ourselves, sometimes we cannot make it work.

Millicent has one son-in-law with whom she gets along very well. Her relationship with her two daughters-in-law is less ideal. Millicent said she must "keep my mouth shut because the fear is always present that I will offend or be taken the wrong way." She feels she cannot be open with one of her daughters-in-law who whispers behind her back and tells "untruths." The other daughter-in-law has very poor home management skills. But, in the end, Millicent stated both marriages are strong and that's what is really important.

~ ~ ~

Beth said she has to be very careful with her choice of words when talking to her daughter-in-law. "She [daughter-in-law] can say anything she wants to me with no regard to my feelings. I have had to walk a wide circle around her for eight years now, and weigh my words carefully. She speaks to me in a manner saying hurtful things that I would never say to anyone. My husband and I mostly communicate through our son, not only in regard to the welfare of the grandchildren but in the manner she treats him as well. My husband tried to have a sensitive private conversation with our daughter-in-law about her impact on the family." Beth said this was a mistake. Her daughter-in-law blames everyone else for the strained relationship and has been cool to her husband and her ever since. Suggestions are taken as a personal attack.

~ ~ ~

Zoe, a teacher, said, "I never share with our sons my frustrations relating to their wives' behavior. When we are with our sons and their families everyone makes an effort to be pleasant." Zoe works on maintaining a harmonious relationship with the two daughters-in-law while feeling disappointed in their lack of sensitivity toward her. Even more hurtful, Zoe feels they have inadequate mothering skills. Both depend on nannies to raise their children; both hold very competitive positions in the corporate world. They are rarely at home. As a teacher, Zoe is very sensitive to the developmental needs of growing children, in this case, her own grandchildren.

Zoe said, "I consider them thorough WIMPS in the housekeeping and parenting departments! (There I've said it and I'm glad!)" However, Zoe said her sons seem content. Zoe has settled for whatever time and influence is available to her, but she worries.

Sometimes all we can do is the best we can do. Sometimes it's good to know that we are not alone. Mothers-in-law sometimes do suffer, and usually in silence. The underlying threat is that we may lose contact with our own children and our grandchildren. It's an uneven power structure.

However, silence can sometimes make a bad situation worse. Often barriers are erected on both sides out of fear and/or lack of trust. Most mothers-in-law want the same things. We want our children and grandchildren to be happy. We want to be a part of their lives. And, if we are to be healthy and wise, we want to have lives of our own, independent of our grown children. The more we live our lives and work on ourselves, the more we will have to give and the more likely what we have to give will be accepted.

Another group of women took a slightly more assertive position.

Sheila said sometimes it's very hard to stay out of in-law situations when you see a need to protect your children. "I try very hard to stay out of these problems unless I am asked, and if I am, I tell them but don't expect them to abide by my advice."

~ ~ ~

Sherry, a hospital administrator, has two daughters-in-law and one ex-daughter-in-law. With her experience, she has learned "If my children ask for advice, I *might* give it. It all depends what they're asking. I may suggest one adult child do something and this may go against what they really want to do and they'll hold it against me. So I listen to anything they have to tell me but there are times I will not tell them what I think. This way, I'm not upsetting anyone. Sometimes when they speak their concerns out, they themselves will make their own decision. I will help them as much as I can when they've made their decision, but it is *their* decision..." Sherry goes on to say, "My husband sometimes feels he should tell the children what to do. He may even take issue with 'a grain of sand' but he rarely succeeds." Sherry feels you have to treat others the way you wish to be treated, and give others the right to learn their own lessons.

~ ~ ~

Rose, a childbirth educator, finds it especially challenging responding to her adult children and their spouses when they sometimes ask and want her opinion, and, at other times, they may ask for an opinion BUT, she says, they really don't want it! Trying to figure out the difference and keeping her mouth shut can be daunting.

There are some ways to clarify situations such as Rose describes. Sometimes you can be straightforward and ask, "Do you really want my opinion or are you just thinking out loud?" Another, more subtle approach is to pay close attention to your grown child's responses. Does his or her expression change, eyes gloss over? Is there a slight pull back from you? Does he or she begin to talk before you are finished? If so, it's time to *stop, look and listen*. If, however, your child moves slightly toward you and/or asks questions, you are probably on the right track.

Iris, a nurse, tries very hard to hold her tongue. Her own mother did and she feels she benefited from that example and wants to do this with her own children. The main issue for her that makes it hard not to interfere is the discipline (or lack thereof) of the grandchildren. She feels their parents are too indulgent, especially her daughter-in-law. The grandchildren are "picky and self-centered." When they stay with her a week or more, these behaviors disappear, until the parents return. She sometimes does talk to her son, but nothing changes.

~ ~ ~

Lee, an educator, and her husband have taken the position from the beginning of each child's marriage that "It is their turn, not ours. What decisions they make and how and where they choose to live their lives is their business." If asked, Lee may offer an opinion but, in general, their position is to "butt out and mean it." They have freedom to reestablish their life and also the freedom to do what they want to do again. Their motto is, "Be there and be helpful when needed, but be quiet."

It is clear that these women are picking their way through the thicket. Central to these stories is that the mothers-in-law were included in the family decision-making process. They appear to be respected and trusted. The fact that their advice may or may not be taken is immaterial. They felt heard and included.

We would be remiss if we did not include an example of one mother-in-law who got it wrong. In this instance, things went completely off track. We never advocate saying whatever you want, whenever you want, without regard to feelings or propriety. Once the trust base is blown, it is very hard to regain it.

Alice cut off her nose to spite her face. She unrestrainedly put her opinions front and center. She destroyed her relationship with her son, his wife, and the grandchildren. Eventually, her son sent her a letter outlining all the reasons his family was cutting her out of their lives. She no longer sees her grandchildren at all. She believes since she is older and wiser, her family should have listened to and followed her advice. She now stands alone, alienated from her family.

In the following vignettes, women have shared some of the methods they have worked out in order to keep the lines of communication open, maintain a positive relationship with their adult children and spouses and still keep themselves honest and authentic.

Anne, a bus driver, lives with her daughter and son-in-law. She prays for wisdom and strength to be there for her family, all the while staying "aloof" from their affairs. At the same time, Anne tries to be helpful and balance each situation that arises with love and understanding and keep everyone on the same page if she can. She walks a fine line. "Never let the lines of communication break down, and love your family unconditionally. Keep a good sense of humor while letting them make their own mistakes. What more could a mother or grandmother want but to maintain a happy family? The rewards are endless and you end up getting more than you could ask for."

~ ~ ~

Muriel, a homemaker, has found she doesn't worry as much about offending her son-in-law as she does her daughter-in-law. Muriel believes that "Men have thicker skins. Also, I can say things to my daughter because I am more important to her life than I am to my daughter-in-law. I work very hard to be extremely positive and supportive of my daughter-in-law. After a number of goofs, I think I learned not to be critical or bossy, but I'm not perfect so I slip up from time to time. We let our daughter-in-law know how dear she is to us and we always want her to be safe and protected. We try to do this without smothering her."

~ ~ ~

Ivy, an administrative assistant and editor, finds it daunting not to be judgmental or critical of any actions that her daughter-in-law takes that she does not agree with, especially in the rearing of the children. "I try to walk lightly in that area and discuss only those elements I feel are too serious to ignore...Because of her trust, I feel I can speak if some action of the children is worrisome to me. But I try to keep any discussion of this sort to a minimum. I am always aware of a motto I learned in the Navy during the war: 'Loose lips sink ships.' It applies to people. Loose lips can sink a relationship, so I keep mine tightly closed

during any tense moments. I have to walk a
fine line."

~ ~ ~

Patricia, a special education teacher,
tries not to give too much unsolicited advice
and accepts that her children have their way
of doing things and tries not to be critical.
Patricia makes a point to call and talk with
them to maintain communication.

~ ~ ~

Bettina, an engineer, offers advice only
when asked. Bettina has learned to step back
and substantially alter the parenting behavior
she used for so many years. She has
discovered treating her daughters and their
husbands as *friends* works best for her.
Bettina recommends biting your tongue from
time to time. Encouraging strong family
bonding by scheduling frequent family
dinners, arranging to celebrate special
occasions together and sponsoring family
vacations from time to time works for her. In
a sense, Bettina is still "engineering," but she
has worked out a rhythm and routine that is
acceptable to all and which feels manipulative to none.

The issues surrounding mothers-in-law
keeping their mouths shut are complex. There are
at least two areas that require attention. First, it is

important for our children and their spouses to live their own lives. Decisions such as where they will live, what they buy, how they spend money and so forth are entirely within their control. Adult children need to make their way in the world, doing what they like, making and learning from their mistakes, just as we did.

Second, and perhaps more important, is how and when to speak up. If something is said or done that is hurtful or harmful, then it is important to speak up and speak up early in order to restore balance. Silence isn't always golden. The goal of speaking up is not to change behaviors (unless they are life threatening); rather, the goal is to get the feelings on the table, work through them and then move on. When you have your say, it must be done carefully and with love. The "I" message technique is easy to learn (see Appendix B) and can often facilitate better understanding. Your adult children may not act upon what you say or behave the way you would wish, but you will have kept yourself whole and balanced—you will be taking care of yourself.

Chapter Eight
Out To Lunch...Or What?!

The hottest places in hell are reserved
for those who in time of great moral crisis
maintain their neutrality.

—Dante Alighieri

 A certain amount of restructuring and redefining family roles before, during and after a wedding is to be expected. However, when the new structures are in place and mothers-in-law are left feeling hurt, confused, abandoned and/or rejected, something is out of balance.

Early on, before her son married, Sybil, a dressmaker/tailor, and her husband found themselves excluded from the wedding plans. After the wedding, they were not invited to over half the holidays the family had always celebrated together. Sybil recalled that she had a great relationship with her son and wanted her daughter-in-law to be close. "I did all I could: I helped financially, did lots of dressmaking for my daughter-in-law, and babysat, but it hasn't helped at all." Sybil's husband concluded they shouldn't interfere; the couple needed to get on with their lives. In spite of feeling hurt, she did just that.

Sybil was in a serious car accident and received no contact from her son and his family. After her husband died, the amount of contact became even less frequent. Sybil said it has been hard to watch her friends having warm relationships with their families while she does not. So Sybil travels a lot, which helps her forget that she has no family life.

~ ~ ~

Nancy talks about her difficult daughter-in-law who rejects contact with her and even rejects her gifts to the grandson if they don't meet with her strict criteria. When the baby was born, Nancy spent her vacations babysitting, but the daughter-in-law always complained about something Nancy touched or moved or threw away when she was there. When she visits now, she is not allowed to cook or clean and so just does nothing. Nancy says, "It has been challenging to accept that I just don't have any rights: my relationship with my son and grandson is wholly in my daughter-in-law's hands." Nancy goes on to say, "I am at the end of my rope…I am at the point of just not having a relationship with them at all."

There is sadness and despair in the stories of Sybil and Nancy. There can be mistakes and hurt feelings in any relationship. However, why don't these sons support their mothers at all? And how do we, as mothers, cope with the loss of our sons? There are times when women come to the realization that enough is enough! Life does not and should not revolve around our children for our entire lives. If we are not welcomed by our grown children, it's not healthy for us to be part of that negativity. And moping around, wringing our hands and shedding tears will not change what is. It's time to take a deep breath, look around and take control of the only life we have.

It's also time to open up to all the possibilities in life that are available once the children are grown and gone. Sybil travels, Nancy continues to work. In addition to those activities, Sybil and Nancy, and others in more or less the same situation, need to enlarge their support systems. Counseling services are available, often at a sliding scale for people who may not otherwise be able to afford it. There are self-help groups that can help people work through their feelings. Classes at community colleges are available to inspire and help refocus lives.

Peggy noted that her daughter-in-law is jealous and resents any relationship that her son might have with his friends or work friends. Peggy also stated that her daughter-in-law lacks compassion for her son, his daughters from a previous marriage, or his family. This daughter-in-law did not permit the grandchildren to visit Peggy on Thanksgiving or Christmas; the daughter-in-law also refused to come, and Peggy's son was not allowed to bring the children. Sometimes her son visits or calls; most of the time he stays with his wife and children.

~ ~ ~

Gale and her husband are not allowed to babysit their granddaughter or buy her holiday gifts. They do not want to rock the boat so they have agreed to accept the relationship on the daughter-in-law's terms. It is better to have something of a relationship than nothing at all. Gail concluded: "I try not to feel too left out...to realize they prefer being around others more than they do us."

How does this happen? Did some of us raise WIMPS?

Sally has a master's degree, teaches full time and travels during the summers with her husband. They have a son and daughter-in-law and two grandchildren living with them. Sally maintains she is not an intrusive or controlling person; she is busy with her own life. Sally believes another daughter-in-law, who lives out of town, is very possessive of her other son. This daughter-in-law refuses to attend family gatherings, tries to win all other family members to her side, and keeps the grandchildren away by leaving the house with the children when family gatherings occur. Sally asks us to pray for mothers-in-law everywhere, and for her to handle this situation carefully.

~ ~ ~

Linda said her daughter-in-law takes good care of her son but keeps him dependent and is rude and disrespectful to her. Linda said her husband worked hard to understand what is "eating their daughter-in-law, and has been most kind and helpful to her." Nonetheless, they found that when the couple moved out of state, the relationship deteriorated even further. Linda and her husband visited the couple for one week and stayed at a hotel. Her daughter-in-law was basically critical and rude throughout the visit.

These mothers-in-law deserve better! It is very difficult to understand what is happening here. What have these mothers done that they should be pushed aside and separated from their sons? More importantly, *where are their sons*? How did their sons, babies who were nourished, boys who were attended to, young men who were objects of pride and joy, become so alienated from the source of their being? All the blame cannot fall on the daughters-in-law. Sons need to be made aware of the imbalance, maybe need to be reminded about who they are and where they came from. At the same time, mothers-in-law need to pull back, stop grieving and rebuild their lives, perhaps recapturing dreams that were put aside before there were sons who needed so much of them. None of this is easy, but it is essential that we rebuild our lives and regain our balance.

The following stories focus on mothers-in-law who are beginning the rebuilding process.

One daughter-in-law out of three is difficult for June, who said this daughter-in-law "does not hold her own in helping to support the family, always argues with my son when I am with them, and is a very sloppy housekeeper." June noted that despite challenges with the one daughter-in-law, all three sons have wonderful families who respect her for what she has done as a parent. She said if asked, she will give advice, and added, "My husband and I both love being empty-nesters. It is great to see the children, but we have made a wonderful life for ourselves doing things we could not do when they were young."

~ ~ ~

Bonnie's son seems content with his life and Bonnie acknowledges that his wife has introduced him to a whole new dimension of happiness. However, Bonnie thinks her daughter-in-law is painfully insecure and uncomfortable outside the comfort zone of her own home. When the four of them are together, her husband is with her son and she is with her daughter-in-law working to establish a good relationship. Bonnie said "the effort is very hard work and emotionally exhausting, sort of like talking to a brick wall." Her son said in the future, his wife may not be joining him when he visits. Bonnie and her husband see this as "problematic and wish it weren't this way." She said she finds herself not wanting to be a mother-in-law. "Can't I just be my son's mother?"

New family relationships often, if not always, bring about complications that we cannot avoid. The positive part of Bonnie's story is that their son wants to continue to have a relationship with his parents. Perhaps the visits should move to their daughter-in-law's comfort zone or a neutral zone such as a restaurant and be time limited. That way, Bonnie and her husband could try to analyze what their daughter-in-law needs. If she needs security, then it might be good to move in her direction for a while. If there's more going on, moving in her direction would be one way to try to uncover what else is happening. Sometimes what we assume to be the problem turns out to be something else entirely.

Madeline has three sons and three daughters-in-law. One son is married to the "Queen of Disharmony." Her son does not discuss his wife with Madeline. This daughter-in-law verbally attacked her in public. Further, this daughter-in-law constantly found fault and was totally disrespectful to her. While they have good relationships with their other daughters-in-law, Madeline and her husband are now completely estranged from this one. However, their son does visit every other week along with his children, and the grandparents have a great time with them. Without the daughter-in-law everyone is more relaxed. Madeline said after years of working on the relationship, she is at peace with this arrangement.

We note with pleasure that Madeline's son did not deny himself or his children an ongoing relationship with his parents. While we can understand how such an arrangement came to be, there is something sad about this house divided. It gives us heart to remember nothing is forever, though, and things may change for the better in the future.

Call it a lack of understanding, poor communication, distrust, or the inability to put yourself in someone else's place: when creating new families and reconstructing old ones, hurt and anger can occur instantly and take years to work out. If it is to be worked out, it is important that all parties come together for resolution; everyone must take a seat at the table. If not, then life in the extended family will continue along the same course, and each member will need to make the best of it.

A mobile cannot be balanced if one piece continues to dodge and weave. If it seems you cannot immediately resolve the issues that create heartache in your family, keep in mind that you are in control of your life, and only your life. Take charge, use your energy constructively. Turn away from your hurt and turn toward building the rest of your life exactly the way you choose.

Chapter Nine

Here We Go Again

When a child is born, so is a grandmother.
—Judith Levy

 Grandparent-hood can provide an avenue for legitimate involvement in the lives of married children and strengthen ties which may have been weakened at the "empty nest" transition. Grandparent-hood presents an opportunity for the new parents and the grandparents to become re-involved as they focus together on the newest family member's life. This shared love can strengthen relationships, with the baby providing the momentum for this rebuilding to begin.

Child development theory tells us it is in the best interests of kids to have their grandparents in their lives, even if the situation isn't perfect. Sometimes it may take a good deal of effort and forbearance but if this is achieved, the whole family stands to gain in the end: everyone wins.

When grandchildren enter our family mobile, everything shifts and changes. It is a time of high emotion, joy and happiness. These tiny babies, so dependant and so lovable, bring back all the feelings that we had when our own children were born. As grandmothers, we want to have a part in their lives, to have them be a part of our lives.

There are situations, however, when efforts are not reciprocated...and sometimes are even rejected. The only option may be to remain open and patient. Remember, nothing is forever. We all acknowledge that brooding and resentment are counter-productive and serve only to harm ourselves. Far better to simply wait for an opening to work it through again. In the meantime, continue to explore and enjoy all the positive and productive aspects of your life.

Lindsay's comments illustrate this point.

Lindsay has a daughter-in-law who punishes her by not letting her see her granddaughter if she does something her daughter-in-law doesn't like. Lindsay stated, "I have searched the Web for support. I am a very level-headed person. I know the mother-in-law/daughter-in-law relationship is a hard one. I had a difficult mother-in-law but I worked on my husband's family until they accepted me. I loved my husband enough to make it work. When my husband's parents died, they felt like I was one of their own. The trend today seems to be that daughters-in-law should be catered to. If the mother-in-law doesn't fall into step with her needs, then the mother-in-law is the villain. It just isn't always true."

While times and perspectives change for all of us, there is one condition etched in stone on which we would all agree. Holding grandchildren hostage, subject to the vagaries of a parent, is inexcusable (unless, of course, there is an abuse issue).

A new baby can, obviously, upset the family balance for a while. Every generation develops new ideas about the right way to raise children which may be quite different or at odds with our own. This new generation has very fluid ideas about roles of parents and, most likely, grandparent roles, too. Some of these ideas may be emotionally charged. Unresolved issues with in-laws are likely to re-emerge and intensify when grandchildren arrive, and sometimes stretch relationships to the breaking point. There is a lot of opportunity for conflict and everyone is on new ground. What one daughter-in-law perceives as being offered help, another may perceive as intrusive and critical behavior on the part of a mother-in-law.

Marianne and her husband, who is CEO of a large company, are forced to deal only with their son regarding their two grandchildren. Their births have made the uneasy relationship with their daughter-in-law even more so. Marianne believes anything she says relating to her grandchildren is seen by her daughter-in-law as an attack on her "mothering" abilities. The son and his family no longer visit because these grandparents have not hired a firm to childproof their home. Wendy said she raised her own children with common sense and vigilance and objects to spending $2,000 for this service, which she regards as unnecessary. Further, the couple own dogs, and their daughter-in-law maintains that the children are allergic to dogs. She blames the children's upper respiratory infections on the dogs even though family visits are rare and, when Grandma and Grandpa do come to visit, they are required to shower, wash their hair and wear fresh clothes before they come.

Not only do the above problems interfere with family harmony, Marianne reported that her daughter-in-law speaks to her in hurtful ways and says things "I would never say to anyone." Clearly, this is an untenable situation for Marianne and her husband, but they must cater to the daughter-in-law's demands or face the possibility of not seeing their grandchildren at all.

Maria is a therapist with one grandchild whose innocent presence has pulled the family apart more than pulled them together. Her daughter married a man who is very controlling and disrespectful to Maria. Even so, there continued to be some contact between Maria and her daughter. When the grandchild arrived, the paternal grandparents became very involved and possessive. Over time, Maria withdrew from her daughter's family and concluded that while she is pleased to be a grandmother, she doesn't have a role in her daughter's family life. Given the circumstances, Maria has chosen to step back, preferring to avoid even greater hurt and discomfort for her daughter, grandchild and herself.

~ ~ ~

Dora, also a therapist, is very concerned about the way her grandchildren are being raised. She told us that both parents are highly educated and very successful financially. The grandchildren, in Dora's opinion, are "materialistic, domineering and disrespectful of their own brilliant (and stupid) parents." Dora said the parents don't treat each other with respect which she feels gives the children license to do the same. She finds it hard to abide her grandchildren's spoiled, self-centered behavior. Dora believes they are growing up without boundaries and appropriate emotional balance. The parents' money is an influential force which is difficult to counteract. So Dora leaves the family to their own resources. She regrets very much that she has had to renounce the positive impact she might have had on her grandchildren but sees no way to fix this situation.

All three of these grandmothers have a lot to contribute to their grandchildren, but there is little receptivity or appreciation from the parents. All three grandmothers have chosen to withdraw rather than take a more assertive posture.

There are no easy solutions here. These three women weighed facts as they understood them and made conscious decisions to disengage from the pain. By stepping back, they are giving themselves and others a message: *I am in control of myself and what I want to do with my life.* While not always easy, choosing to take the high road is surely much healthier than surrendering your values and your sense of self. In the meantime, situations do change, sometimes even for the better. As Yogi Berra famously commented, "It's never over till it's over."

Sometimes the opposite problem occurs, and a mother-in-law may feel she must put her grown children's and grandchildren's needs before her own—a situation filled with mixed blessings.

When Hannah, a retiree, agreed to take care of her infant grandson, she did not realize she was committing to several years of providing daycare while her son and daughter-in-law worked. Then they decided to have another child. Hannah, unable or unwilling to speak up, reluctantly agreed to care for this new grandson as well. Months stretched into years with no relief in sight. Hannah continued to suffer in silence, torn between her love of her grandsons and the burden of caring for them full time as she aged. The impasse only ended when her son got a new job and the family relocated.

~ ~ ~

Jill, also retired, tells us that she always seems to be in demand for babysitting and would like more time for herself. Although she finds her grandchildren wonderful, caring for them on short notice sometimes spoils personal plans. Not speaking up and stating your own needs can be detrimental to your self-esteem as well as interfere with your own schedule and plans.

Both of these women felt the pressures that come when external forces and internal needs are in conflict. Not wanting to offend and possibly cause a rift in the family, the women chose to suppress their feelings and work instead to please their children. Suppressing feelings rarely works to anyone's benefit. Resentment and anger build until there is, almost inevitably, a blow-up. Far better to think clearly, use some form of an "I" message (see Appendix B), and get your sentiments out on the table.

These incidences of grandmothers who face barriers carrying out their coveted grandmother role represent only part of the story. Other grandmothers have positive experiences to share.

Sally, a social worker, tells us, "My grandchildren have completed the cycle of my life: they are the reason for family and marriage. My daughter-in-law is a wonderful mother, my son is a wonderful dad, and they've managed to raise two great sons who are a joy to be around. They do well in school and respect people's rights and property. Earlier I felt my son and daughter-in-law were a little too strict in their upbringing of the boys but the results speak for themselves. On the couple of occasions when I interfered, both my son and daughter-in-law later confided to me that I was right and rescinded a punishment, but advised the boys that it was because Grandma spoke up for them."

Sally is a seasoned grandmother. She was able to talk with her son and daughter-in-law about her concerns and they were mature and confident enough within themselves to be willing to listen and adjust their behavior. Not only that, these parents were willing to give Sally credit for their reversal. What wonderful communication. No one felt threatened, no one got defensive, and the situation was resolved to everyone's satisfaction, especially the boys'.

One of the most delightful and inspirational stories we came across in our research was that of Margie, a grandmother and former preschool teacher.

Camp Sugar Cereal is an annual event for grandchildren hosted by Margie, where each summer, six grandchildren come to stay with her for a week. The day begins, you guessed it, with a large variety of sugar cereals... the kind most parents won't supply for their children at home. Other daily indulgences follow: later bedtimes, extra movie watching, backward dinners. Some of the ideas are Margie's; some are developed by the children as the week progresses.

When "Camp" is over, reentry problems for the children are minimal as everyone understands parents and grandparents have different rules outside of this special week.

In this situation, everyone wins. Margie gets some wonderful time with her grandchildren. Siblings, cousins and grandmother have a bonding experience, and the parents get some time alone, knowing their children are in safe, loving, capable hands. At the end of the week, when readjusting to reality, both parents and children have a smooth landing. We can imagine that Grandma would like a nice, long rest afterward, and maybe a martini to celebrate another successful "camp season."

Margie began a unique and fun-filled tradition so she could bond with her grandchildren. We each have to think of ways that allow us to relate to our grandchildren on our own terms. Unrealistic expectations from either parents or grandparents can cause painful family problems. No matter how much pressure you get, it is important not to fall into a preconceived grandparent role that doesn't fit you. Otherwise, your grandchildren, your children and spouses, and most of all you, are not likely to be happy. Remember, be proud of the type of grandmother you are. Not all of us can deliver on cookie baking, babysitting and Camp Sugar Cereal, even though we might like to. We each have to blaze our own grandparent path.

After the birth of a grandchild, women are more likely to increase contact with their mothers, re-establishing an intimacy not shared as fully with their mothers-in-law. Most mothers consider grandmothers to be the best source of childcare, although there is, in most cases, a preference for their own mother. Both sides of the family are generally involved when grandchildren arrive. However, mothers are more likely to do things and mothers-in-law are more likely to buy things.

Sometimes maternal grandmothers may be no more willing to become mother substitutes than paternal grandparents but feel obligated to accept this responsibility even though they prefer not to. Dave Barry, the humorist, commented, "The best baby sitters, of course, are the baby's grandparents. You feel completely comfortable entrusting your baby to them for long periods, which is why most grandparents flee to Florida."

Elise told us her grandchildren have drawn the family closer and given her children greater insight into the real priorities of life. She said her grandchildren have brought her great joy; it is something she cannot easily put into words, saying, "We all have to experience it for ourselves."

~ ~ ~

Madison, a teacher, does not live close to her grandchildren but she talks to them often. "Aren't cell phones great?" she asked. Madison enjoys talking with her college-age grandson and the two-year-old grandson. She conceded the younger one probably doesn't know who she is yet, but talking to him is still fun for her.

~ ~ ~

Anna, an artist, has a perspective on becoming a grandmother that says it all. "When I first learned my daughter was expecting a baby, I had a profound sense that I was part of a long river of life that went before me and would extend when my life was over. I found the connection to that river immensely comforting. In a sense, I felt I had contributed to the continuous regeneration of humankind, that I had completed one of God's most essential and joyous tasks. Becoming a grandmother put a wondrous perspective on life that I could not have imagined before the baby was born."

What Sets Us Apart
A Few More Gnarly Problems

The following chapters discuss five of the most common secondary challenges that tend to disrupt in-law relationships.

Chapter Ten
Rejection

Human beings, like plants,
grow in the soil of acceptance,
not in the atmosphere of rejection.

—John Powell

 It is very painful when a daughter-in-law rejects her mother-in-law out of hand. Most of the time, the rejection has little, if anything, to do with the mother-in-law herself.

In the following stories, several mothers-in-law share their experiences with rejection, and later in the chapter we will discuss some ways to cope or at least begin to make peace with situations we can't change.

Justine said cigarettes became the excuse that her daughter-in-law used to begin her rejection. Whenever Justine came to visit, her daughter-in-law went outside to smoke. In addition, whenever her daughter-in-law invited Justine over, as soon as she would show up, so would her daughter-in-law's mother or sister or both. Justine said it was as if the young woman needed the "barrier" of her own family whenever Justine was there.

Additionally, whenever there was a family gathering at the daughter-in-law's, she and her immediate family would get cozy in the kitchen, but as soon as Justine came in, the conversation would stop. There was no effort to include or welcome her. So Justine developed the strategy of staying in the living room with her grandchildren until it was time to leave.

~ ~ ~

Rebecca's daughter-in-law divorced her son and then they remarried. Rebecca said that in between the first and second marriage, her daughter-in-law was pleasant. However, that all changed, beginning with the second wedding. Rebecca's daughter-in-law would not allow her in-laws to attend the second marriage service. Later she would not allow her mother-in-law to attend her baby shower or even see her grandchild. Both Rebecca and her gifts were totally rejected. Now Rebecca believes that the between-marriage pleasantness was part of her daughter-in-law's manipulation to get her husband back, and once she accomplished that she reverted to her old behaviors. Rebecca's question is how to get along with someone who wants nothing to do with you.

~ ~ ~

Kathy's son and daughter-in-law live some eight hundred miles away. Kathy said, "I would love a loving and close relationship with my daughter-in-law. I live far away and don't understand why everything I do has a negative impact. I have been told not to buy anything for their house because they do not want to feel obligated to use it. Younger girls I work with love their mothers-in-law to take them shopping. It's a shame because I have the means to help, but she wants no part of it. She told me ten times after she received a toy in the mail that my grandson liked the box better. They have only been to visit me twice in five years."

~ ~ ~

Maria said that she always wanted to be the best mother-in-law. She wanted to be a support to her daughter-in-law and help her feel good about herself. Maria said, "It's a great shock to find out that sometimes no matter how loving and understanding you might be, your daughter-in-law wants to reject and dislike you for reasons known only to her."

Experiencing rejection is hurtful—no question about it. And there are no easy solutions. However, the only emotions and feelings we can control are our own. We can work to clear the air. Strive to have an honest, open discussion about feelings and offer to talk matters through or even begin again with a clean slate. Sometimes, even with all the skills and desires we have at our disposal, the rejection continues. In those cases, it is best to pull back and not put ourselves in a position to continue to be hurt.

One definition of insanity is doing the same thing over and over and expecting a different result. Change your behavior, do what feels right to you, and keep the door open for whatever change of heart may happen.

Of all the stories we received, the following was one of the most poignant.

Thirty years ago, immediately after their divorce, Paula's ex-husband married her younger sister, and Paula's two children went to live with this ex-husband and her sister (now the children's stepmother as well). Quite a complex family structure! Eventually the children married and there are several grandchildren in the picture. Paula's children and their spouses make some effort to keep the attention balanced between Paula and her sister but it does put a strain on everyone.

Paula sometimes feels that her sons have forgotten they have a biological mother, and the sons' wives are not as welcoming as she would hope.

"The daughters-in-law have replaced me. Neither son shows much interest in what I am doing or in helping me in any way." Her daughters-in-law show very little warmth or enthusiasm for her and do not express appreciation for her gifts for them or their children. With all of this rejection, Paula still says, "I am happy that my children have happy, stable homes." Paula's solution to her situation is to spend much of her time with friends. She reads, sings in the choir, and attends church functions.

Considering Paula's experience with betrayal and trauma, she is doing very well. She has created a life for herself and has adjusted to her circumstances. Paula acknowledges, respects and appreciates her children's lives. It would be nice if, over the years, the families could move closer to one another, but sometimes life does not cooperate to create such a happy ending.

Sometimes, if we are lucky and all parties are healthy and cooperative, we can find a way to overcome rejection. We end this chapter with a positive tale from one of the many women who wrote to us with their stories.

Edith recalls that she learned to be a mother-in-law thirty years ago when her son married a young woman whose mother was a perfectionist. This mother always criticized her daughter so she had little self-confidence by the time she got married. This daughter-in-law became very possessive, did not want her husband anywhere near his mother, did not want her husband to even wear a gift shirt if it was from her mother-in-law.

Edith's son explained the situation to his mother, calling from work because his wife did not like him calling from home. Edith took it upon herself to convince her daughter-in-law that she "didn't bite." She called her daughter-in-law with invitations to dinner, praised her for everything she did or made, and never made comparisons. By the time the second grandchild arrived, Edith's daughter-in-law wanted her help, not her mother's, and now they are good friends. Edith said her daughter-in-law will call and say, "Mom, I miss you. I need to hear your cheery voice."

Edith worked hard to achieve this obviously successful and loving relationship. She deserves her success.

Chapter Eleven
Communication

*The ability to repeat what other family members
have said is one of the most dangerous weapons
lying around the house.*

—Deborah Tannen

 Communication can cover a variety
of situations, including but not
limited to regional and/or cultural
diversities, generational differences, male/female
styles, listening skills, expectations and
assumptions, body language, and personal
historical experiences. Tannen (2001) states the
following: "All families are like cross-cultural
experiences in that each partner was born into a
particular family and every family is, in a way, a
nation unto itself, with its own customs and ways
of speaking."

In earlier times, people generally married
locally. Now, we tend to be multi-state or even
global in our choice of mate. It's easy to
understand how miscommunication can arise,

especially at times of stress such as a wedding, holiday decisions and babies.

Very often, where generations are involved, the slights and hurts are not intentional. For example, the mother-in-law generation worries about security, represented by a home, food and clothing for the family and a "nest egg" for financial security. The adult children may be more concerned about living in the right neighborhood, owning the latest electronic gear, taking exciting vacations, and ensuring good child care.

Miscommunication between the sexes is legendary! For example, many women discuss what is troubling them with friends. Talking about personal problems, taking inside information about the family outside, is one of the fundamental ways women create friendships. Women form close bonds by sharing themselves and trusting their close friends. Men often perceive this as betrayal: they don't see the purpose and resent the exposure. Men's friendships, for the most part, are built on sharing activities, not on sharing details of their lives.

When a mother-in-law feels rejection due to a lack of communication with her daughter-in-law, hurt feelings often ensue. There are so many ways to say what we want to say and just as many ways to have what we say misinterpreted.

Pat feels some bitterness toward her daughter-in-law who is reluctant to talk to her on the phone and does not invite her to the home she shares with Pat's son. Further, when it comes to gift-giving, her daughter-in-law "Puts her two cents in on her choice of gifts for my son."

~ ~ ~

Sara has one daughter-in-law, with whom communication is difficult. She said her daughter-in-law gets insulted when she makes any suggestions. An additional source of hurt for Sara is that her daughter-in-law prefers to pay a babysitter rather than allow Sara to provide child care. This has made the relationship worse. Sara said she feels lost and has little contact with her son and daughter-in-law or her grandchild. "I just wonder what they are doing, why I am standing outside their lives."

The two women in the preceding stories have been unable to find a way to bridge the chasm between themselves and their daughters-in-law. Although the plight of these women, and many others with similar stories, appears difficult or even insurmountable, there are ways to bring greater equanimity to the relationship. We discuss several strategies in Part III.

Many women we surveyed continue to work on communication with their daughters-in-law, recognizing it as a basic challenge that needs attention. They also recognize that the rewards are tremendous when even small breakthroughs occur.

Monica observed that her insecure daughter-in-law "brags about herself without anything to brag about." She can't seem to accomplish what she sets out to do. The family tiptoes around her and doesn't call attention to the fact that her efforts don't materialize into reality.

Monica's attempts to communicate with this daughter-in-law are basically not to communicate, not to say anything. When appropriate, Monica offers sympathy when something goes wrong, praise when something is even moderately positive and does not volunteer any opinion or advice. Monica said, "I would love to be closer to my daughter-in-law but I think her insecurities do not allow her to be open with me. We get along best when I talk about how bright and clever and wonderful her daughter is."

In Monica's situation, she is working hard to keep the doors wide open and connect with her daughter-in-law. Her story highlights the fact that communication has to be a two-way street. It is very difficult to work things through, to have an open and honest talk when only one party is willing to participate. There are, as we know, two sides to every story and Monica's daughter-in-law may have quite a different account of their interactions. Still, until such time as her daughter-in-law is able to come willingly to the table, Monica is left to draw her own conclusions and interpretations and act as she feels best.

The relationship between mothers-in-law and daughters-in-law appears to be more sensitive than other relationships. Realistic or not, there is always the fear of being perceived as critical. Perhaps these hesitancies, with care and nurturing, can be alleviated over time.

Loraine stated when she is in her daughter's home, she thinks nothing of stepping in and doing things. In her daughter-in-law's home, however, it is different. Loraine feels she has to stop, think, and ask before she does things. She does not want to offend her daughter-in-law or have her think she is not doing things right. Loraine's goal is to provide help or guidance when it is needed and in a manner that will not be interpreted as offensive. This way of operating has proved successful for Loraine and she is hopeful that, over time, she can have the same level of comfort that she has with her own daughter.

Some mothers-in-law prefer to stand back, often out of fear that anything else will cause a disturbance in the relationship.

Lindy, a special education teacher, takes a philosophic view of her relationship with her daughter-in-law. They live far away from each other and her daughter-in-law doesn't initiate communication. Lindy said, "She is not naturally a warm person but is very nice." For Lindy, the bottom line is her daughter-in-law makes her son very happy. She believes if your daughter-in-law is a good, decent person, you love her unconditionally if she makes your child happy. "Your child's happiness in the marriage is the most important thing. Hopefully, love on your terms will come later."

One of the greatest ironies of family life is that our family members are our greatest source of comfort and our greatest source of pain. They see our strong points as we wish them to, but they also see our faults. Coming together, working on communicating in ways that are loving and supportive, will go a long way toward breaking down barriers, creating harmony and building more inclusive relationships.

Chapter Twelve
Substance Abuse

The open secrets.
Everybody knows about them and nobody
is supposed to know that everybody knows.
—John Bradshaw

 This book does not presume to offer a treatise on substance abuse; however, a brief introduction will provide the context for the stories that follow.

Sharon Wegscheider, in her book, *Another Chance* (1981), states that: "Fundamentally, the family is a system, just as a machine or a human body is. In the interests of their own personal survival, the members of the family assume behavior patterns that will maintain a balance (homeostasis) in the system. A distorted balance, such as occurs when one member starts becoming dependent on a chemical, causes psychological and/or biological symptoms in the other members."

Often, when substance abuse is involved in a child's marriage, parents are at a loss as to how to proceed. The question of when to say something and what to say is truly a dilemma. Is any interference warranted? If so, how much, when and where? Several of our respondents indicated that if they had known then what they know now, they would have intervened in their adult child's life sooner. As we discuss later in this chapter, being informed and having appropriate support before attempting an intervention is vital if you are to succeed in helping your child.

Jen, a housewife, has a daughter who married a man who had been married three times before. Jen couldn't fathom why her daughter was attracted to this man. He not only had a substance abuse problem, he was an abuser. He isolated her, mistreated her and was very jealous. Jen berates herself for not talking to her daughter enough, instead watching everything get out of hand without expressing her concerns. Her "always be nice and sit back and wait" policy was damaging to her daughter and she regrets that very much.

That marriage ended in divorce. Jen's daughter is now happily remarried to "a very pleasant man who gets along with everyone and has many common interests with the family." Jen says, "He fits into the family like a glove." Having no sons, Jen advised her daughter to marry "someone I can love. Otherwise, how are we all going to get along?"

~ ~ ~

Kate's daughter married a man twenty-five years her senior. She was a "trophy" wife and was, in fact, preceded by four other wives. All five wives, including Kate's daughter, had alcohol problems and dependent personalities. Financially, this man provided luxuries at the drop of a hat and treated Kate's daughter like a princess.

Kate believed that her daughter was seeking a father figure when she married this man. In fact, since he was about the same age as Kate and her husband, they socialized both before and after the marriage. Nearly from the beginning of the relationship, Kate noticed that her daughter's substance use accelerated. Kate's daughter now had almost unlimited access to money and a ready supply of substances, thus exacerbating a preexisting inclination on her part to overuse alcohol and drugs.

According to Kate, her daughter's husband was "extremely co-dependent." In retrospect, Kate is disappointed in herself for failing to intervene. "I should have put my foot down and said what was on my mind." Kate's lifelong laissez faire philosophy got in the way of recognizing her daughter's struggle for what it was. Kate wishes she had been more proactive when it was so necessary.

Eventually, Kate's daughter left her husband and entered a residential rehabilitation program. She later relocated and is now working at a job she loves. We all hope her struggle is behind her.

Jesse had a daughter-in-law who was seriously out of control. Jesse said her daughter-in-law would lie to her son and the family while she was out doing drugs and stripping at a night club. This behavior produced a great deal of pain. Not all situations are capable of being rectified, and this marriage ended. Jesse now second-guesses herself about whether these behaviors could have been observed and/or predicted before the marriage. And if so, would it have made enough of a difference to prevent the marriage? Also, Jesse wonders if she should have seen the signs and done something to help her son and daughter-in-law before it was too late.

Whenever there is substance abuse and anyone intervenes, it is extremely important to proceed with caution. It is critical to gather information from reliable, professional sources as to how to carry out the best, most effective intervention. Often, intervening requires the cooperation of all family members and the help and support of professionals who have experience in the field.

There are risks involved in intervening as well as risks in allowing the status quo. It is critical to carefully weigh both sets of risks before taking any action, because once begun, you cannot backpedal from this chosen course: you only have one chance to stage an intervention. Each case of substance abuse is different, and we cannot stress strongly enough that it is essential to have appropriate professional assistance for your particular situation when considering this potentially life-altering, and lifesaving, action.

Sometimes, families opt to let their children choose their own path and wait and hope for a better tomorrow.

Leah, a single grandmother, had a very difficult mother-in-law who was "selfish, interfering, and demanding." Leah decided now that she is a mother-in-law she would "Keep my mouth shut and just accept they have their own lives." However, Leah has a daughter who is married to a man who uses drugs. He abuses, beats and torments her. Leah sees her grandchildren, who are abused also, as profoundly affected by the passive behavior of their mother and the bullying behavior of their father. Leah, nevertheless, feels she should be polite to her son-in-law "in spite of what I'd like to be." Leah's philosophy is to let go and let God take care of her children.

Leah also speaks of the harmonious and successful relationships she has with her other two children, their spouses, and the grandchildren. She does not see that she has any responsibility to intervene in her one daughter's unfortunate situation. Her solution is to "Just tolerate and stay away." No one else in the family seems inclined to step forward, either.

Sometimes, parents are fortunate enough to catch their children when they are ready to change their behaviors and accept help.

Leslie, a "Jill of all trades," has a daughter who married a man thirty-two years her senior. He was her daughter's drug supplier. Leslie's daughter and son-in-law experienced the worst of all situations that could have brought two people together. Both were into drugs and a lifestyle that was extremely dysfunctional and non-productive except for their own self-gratification. Both people were in and out of jail, with sporadic rehabilitation efforts. Leslie states, "Their latest release from jail was more than a year ago and now I have become my son-in-law's counselor. Communication and trust had to be practiced and judgments overcome." Leslie believes that her son-in-law has transformed his life for her daughter and their infant son. She feels her effectiveness in this situation is due to reassurance and forgiveness when mistakes are made, and being there as a cheerleader.

A serious word of warning is needed here. While it is good to celebrate Leslie's success, generally speaking, acting as a counselor for family members is risky and can lead to disappointment, co-dependency and a host of other unforeseen, unintended consequences. Should you choose to follow Leslie's path, proceed with extreme caution, and never without outside help. Al-Anon would be one excellent source of support.

Chapter Thirteen
Enabling

When your child leaves home to take on adult responsibilities, your parent license expires.

—Elinor Lenz

 An enabler is a person who steps in more frequently, and with increasingly elaborate maneuvering, in an attempt to rescue or protect someone from the consequences of his or her behavior. What constitutes support, and what goes beyond support into a realm from which it becomes increasingly more difficult to exit? Many parents confront this question as they rear their children from infancy right through to adulthood and even beyond.

Nora and her husband worry a great deal about their youngest son, who they acknowledge is spoiled and immature and married to a spoiled and immature woman who was indulged by her parents, too. As time passes in their marriage, they are each frustrated by a long list of personal unmet needs. This has generated anger that is increasingly out of control. Each accuses the other of being responsible for their crumbling marriage and unhappiness. Neither will consider counseling for they each feel if only their partner would submit to anger management classes, their problems would be solved.

Nora feels she must walk on eggshells around them. She watches this marriage deteriorate and observes the negative effect it has on their three grandchildren, and her heart breaks. Nora blames herself for releasing an immature adult into the world. She believes there is nothing she can do except spend as much time as possible with her grandchildren.

Her husband, disgusted with their daughter-in-law's chaotic and slovenly housekeeping, will pitch in and clean their house, do up to ten loads of laundry to regain floor space in the laundry room and bedrooms and then refill the closets with clean, neatly hung or folded clothes. This way when his son comes home from work, he is less likely to be angry. His daughter-in-law is pleased, too—and why shouldn't she be? This must be the ultimate in enabling.

In Nora's situation, it is clear to see the enabling has gotten way out of control. A tsunami will arrive one day and they will all be blown away. Nora's story begs the question: How much is enough? Ten loads of laundry, fifteen, twenty? All of us who have children can easily understand that the enabling process is insidious, and, almost always, begins innocently enough. A little help here and there seems natural, then the help increases and, perhaps, spirals out of control. Over time, enablers will be expected to do more and more in the continued attempt to control or fix the situation. When each attempt at fixing things inevitably fails, the enabler will feel even more ineffective: the behavior continues, both parties trapped in the spin cycle.

Kelly tried over a period of time to respond to the perceived needs of her ex-daughter-in-law, the mother of her beloved granddaughter. The young woman was neither an adequate money manager nor capable of keeping a home with even minimally acceptable sanitation standards. There were animals in the house eating off the sinks and counter tops, stacks of unwashed dishes, and contents of clothes closets on the floor. She was, however, a loving mother. Kelly tried to help by giving them money and by buying things. The dishwasher she bought turned out to be just one more place to stack dirty dishes or leftover food. Kelly made multiple similar efforts, as well. In retrospect, Kelly wonders if her enthusiasm to be helpful to her son and ex-daughter-in-law came across as interference and/or criticism of their personal affairs, and thus was rejected.

Enabling inevitably leads to a downward spiral of powerlessness, anger and more failure. In the end, enabling really does nothing but enable the subjects to continue their inappropriate behaviors, and cause heartache and frustration for the enablers.

Erin has eight children, all but one of whom have happy marriages. However, one daughter-in-law is withdrawn to the point that she is no longer able to attend any family functions. Her husband, Erin's son, comes alone to family events, brings the children, makes excuses for his wife and never acknowledges there is a problem. This daughter-in-law's behavior is becoming noticeably more unusual. The proverbial elephant in the living room is surely present here. It seems ignoring the situation is not the way to resolution.

In Erin's case, the situation is somewhat different than Nora's or Kelly's. No one wants to acknowledge Erin's daughter-in-law's problem. No one wants to "interfere" because, in our society, we are conditioned to mind our own business. However, something is amiss and the entire family is enabling this young woman to continue her behavior. Assuming that Erin's daughter-in-law is not merely avoiding the family because she doesn't like them, she is in some trouble. Her behavior may soon, if it has not already, affect her children. Continuing to ignore, and therefore enable, this behavior will not alleviate this daughter-in-law's suffering.

In all of these stories, a good rule of thumb is to trust your feelings and intuition. If it feels uncomfortable, if you are angry or uneasy, something is probably out of order. Take stock, analyze, get help if you need it, and change your behavior to work toward a happier solution.

Ella, a teacher/artist, has experienced a daughter-in-law becoming too dependent on her for advice and accommodations which she was not really willing or able to give. Ella was wise enough to maintain some distance: "If you don't like your son- or daughter-in-law, you have to learn to like and accept them anyway...but stick by your values and don't enable them or give in to unreasonable requests."

~ ~ ~

Amanda has three ex-daughters-in-law and one current one. Amanda expressed a fear that her daughter-in-law will become dependent on her to try to fix her marriage problems and she will be tied down with their needs. Amanda fears losing some of her freedom and independence, and resists getting sucked into the trap.

Both of these women are using their instincts and experiences to step back and not get pulled into the role of an enabler. Ella said it clearly: "Stick by your values." Amanda sees the pitfalls ahead and is working to steer clear. Whatever challenges lie ahead for their children and respective in-laws will be met by their children and not by them. That is the goal of parenting and the goal of mother-in-lawing as well.

Chapter Fourteen
Mother-in-Law Overboard

One generation cannot bind another.

—Thomas Jefferson

 In Italy, Paola Mescoli Davoli, an Italian lawyer, created a course now widely known as "The Mother-in-Law School." While both wives and mothers-in-law can attend, it is the wives who seem the most emotionally distraught and aggrieved. One participant, a fifty-year-old woman, said that on her first married Christmas, her mother-in-law stated that she'd wanted to give her new daughter-in-law a mink coat, but thought that "this" would be better. "This" turned out to be a prepaid burial plot!

While the vast majority of the situations we discuss in this book tend to be supportive of mothers-in-law, there are cases where mothers-in-law have clearly crossed the line. Sometimes new wives do see their mothers-in-law as a threat or a possible enemy. And sometimes they are. Any mother-in-law who works to control her child when they are grown and married is cheating herself out of the possibility of a mature relationship with the newly formed family. When everyone gets along, life is easier, happier and more fulfilling. The training wheels must come off.

In the spirit of a balanced mother-in-law presentation, and as a cautionary tale, some stories are offered here.

Francie states, "My daughter-in-law seems to make my son happy; however, I do not care about that. I care about my happiness and how my daughter-in-law has taken my son away from me and left me alone. I believe this is true because my daughter-in-law has become number one in our son's eyes. I used to be the one he talked to, visited with, looked to for advice. Now he goes to her. I still wait for my son to see that I am here and realize my daughter-in-law is a distraction from our relationship." Further, Francie perceives her husband as a "traitor" for not standing up for her when their son does not come home, call every night or pay more attention to them. Francie said, "I am really upset that our son has set boundaries that were not there before our daughter-in-law came into the picture."

Francie is suffering and her pain is very real to her, though she hasn't come to terms with reality. When your baby takes his first step, when he enters kindergarten, high school and beyond, there is no turning back the clock. At each stage of a child's development he is preparing for the next stage and moving closer to claiming his independent life. Francie's unwillingness to accept this keeps her trapped in her suffering. Her son is only moving on, not lost forever.

Caroline, a security guard, is accustomed to having control. However, she is often in conflict with her daughter-in-law who is "so unlike us that it's like she is from a foreign country. She's been out of the country and gone to college and her family is pretty wealthy." Caroline's daughter-in-law makes her son happy, "but she really hasn't gotten involved with our family and she will not open up or give way to me." Caroline feels unwelcome when she is told she needs to call before visiting or isn't allowed to cook or clean up after her son. Caroline's daughter-in-law reminds Caroline that she is a guest in their home. Caroline is not allowed to see her grandchild whenever she wants and feels that her daughter-in-law is very territorial about the baby. Her daughter-in-law also reminds her that she and her husband are the parents of the baby, not Caroline. Caroline was upset that she was not allowed in the delivery room when the baby was born.

Apparently, it is Caroline who has boundary issues and it is her daughter-in-law who is capable of giving Caroline straight messages. Caroline is fortunate to have a daughter-in-law who is willing take a stand, set limits and not close off communication completely. If Caroline is to have a continuing relationship with her son, daughter-in-law and grandchild, she needs to understand that setting limits is a healthy way to establish an appropriate division of the families. Caroline's need to have full entree into her son's life is beyond what might reasonably be expected. It is possible that Caroline sees this situation as all or nothing—that is, if Caroline is not totally involved, then there will be nothing for her. It would be helpful if Caroline could step back, listen, and respect her daughter-in-law's limits, and work to reach an understanding of what her new role will be.

Sue Ellen is experiencing difficulty with her new daughter-in-law; however, Sue Ellen's husband gets along very well with her. Sue Ellen, who is a large woman, told the following story.

While visiting her daughter-in-law, whom Sue Ellen describes as "standoffish," Sue Ellen lost it, calling her daughter-in-law "mean and cruel" for putting a *Time* magazine featuring obesity on top of the coffee table.

Sue Ellen acknowledges that she should apologize but feels embarrassed, saying, "She should know I'm sorry and forgive me." Adding to this discomfort is Sue Ellen's account of asking her son and daughter-in-law to loan Sue Ellen and her husband some money. "They must have it, they just bought a new car!" Sue Ellen believes her daughter-in-law is responsible for this refusal. Sue Ellen said, "I think my daughter-in-law is too quick to want to prove herself the matriarch. I'm still the boss."

Sue Ellen is not the boss, nor will she ever have that role again, if she ever did. Sue Ellen appears to have, among other problems, boundary issues. Research tells us that these feelings of loss of control, loss of a place in a child's life, and/or loss of status, can lead to depression and, unless there is an intervention, can lead right back to the pantry for more "comfort." Furthermore, Sue Ellen's unwillingness to apologize for her behavior, even when she recognized that an apology is needed, does not suggest a future conciliation with her daughter-in-law. Having control is not nearly as important as maintaining a healthy, loving relationship with the people who are nearest and dearest to our hearts.

Trudy stated that her only son "always takes his wife's side, no matter what." She feels her son was taken from her and now her daughter-in-law is doing the same by trying to keep Trudy away from the grandchildren. Not only that, her daughter-in-law refuses her gifts and her advice, and Trudy believes "she has no respect for me." Trudy concluded that "All women are born to nurture; both mother and wife want to be the dominant nurturer of the son or husband, and that can be a problem."

Trudy may be partially correct. However, for her to expect that she will always be the "dominant nurturer" of her son is asking for conflict and unhappiness. Giving up center stage is never easy. However, staying too long is even more painful. Now is the time for Trudy to explore the new opportunities that beckon. Maybe dust off some old dreams that were put away while she raised her family.

The road back to her son and daughter-in-law does not lie in the direction she is going. If Trudy has so much nurturing to give, there are many agencies and other outlets that truly need her skills and compassion.

Finally, we offer Mary's story.

Mary is working with honesty through her pain, her feelings of rejection and her jealousy. Mary concedes that her daughter-in-law is the love of her son's life and has brought him happiness through this love and their marriage and child. She also reluctantly concedes that she is no longer the center of her son's life. Mary has a problem accepting that she has been moved aside and has lost control to a younger, more beautiful woman. Mary said she is jealous, and her attitude has caused a rift in family harmony. She has taken ownership of her feelings and understands that she has to take responsibility for resolving her issues. Meanwhile, her family has sidelined her and she has little, if any, contact with her son, his wife, and her grandchild.

Mary has the ability and courage to be honest and accept the blame for her behavior. We believe Mary will prevail and find a way to change her perceptions and move forward with her life. Her family undoubtedly will be waiting for her to turn that corner.

PART III
What Brings Us Together

*The old woman I shall become
will be quite different from the woman I am now.
Another I is beginning.*

—George Sand

Chapter Fifteen
A Time of Renewal

As long as a person is capable of self-renewal,
they are a living being.

—Henri Frederic Amiel

 Think of becoming a mother-in-law as a developmental stage of motherhood. It is an emotional threshold that begins with an awareness of loss and a sense that time is limited. We need to fill the empty spaces which may not include more time with the family. These empty spaces are more apt to include all the things we have neglected in our lives, including dreams and hopes that we put aside for the sake of our family life. And so, at this important juncture of our lives, our spouse, our children and their spouses, and our grandchildren cannot meet all our needs…and why should they? In fact, after the wedding, the new couple wants you to get on with your life as they want to get on with theirs.

Now is your time to recreate a new life on your own terms. Until your child married, you were the center of the family; now, you have been shifted to the periphery. Be joyful. It is a time for renewal, a time to do things there has never been time for before. It is time to assess and rearrange your life. Be aware that many of us have spent more time planning a dinner party than we've spent planning our lives.

One way to begin to make sense of your thoughts is to write in a journal. Long-time journal writers have discovered that getting thoughts down on paper has the power not only to heal, but to pinpoint life's purpose. Any kind of journaling has power because it allows you to relocate things from your head onto the page. The act of writing helps clarify your thoughts and may trigger solutions that would never occur when you're simply mulling something over in your head. The writing process makes room for new thoughts and ideas, and a journal is a wonderful record of where you've been as well as a map for where you want to go.

Your journal may include a way to check yourself out. Some people find journal writing uncomfortable at first. You might want to ease into it by beginning with descriptors. For example, you can talk about your day or the weather, or describe the room in which you are sitting. As the process becomes more familiar, you can go deeper into your thoughts and feelings. At that point, you may begin to ask more relevant questions: *How do I feel about my life at this point? Am I happy? Is there anything missing? Now that I have the opportunity, do I want to turn my life in a different direction? What are the obstacles that occur to me?* Remember, no one will see your journal unless you want them to. This book is truly for your eyes only.

Now, as you gain in self-awareness, imagine you are on a path to make changes happen. The following steps may help to guide you.

Step One: Work on understanding where you want to go and the changes you want to make.

Begin by taking an inventory of your priorities. Plan some short and long term goals. It is important to note that your plan will always be a work in progress and, in fact, may take the rest of your life. However, if you don't begin with a road map, you will probably never arrive at your desired destination. As your journey progresses, so do your dreams, interests and goals. It's a dynamic process and you are the driver.

Step Two: Make a list of all the things you want to do during the rest of your life.

Your list can start with what you do now that makes you feel satisfied and happy.

Continue to list everything you can think of that would bring you pleasure, happiness, and a sense of adventure. Put a check by those items you already do and continue these, and also pick out a new goal.

We know that whenever possible, people naturally choose activities and behaviors that make them feel fully alive, competent, creative, and autonomous. Don't hold back; you're only creating a list for yourself. You may be surprised at what comes off on the page. Be creative and have fun with it. All journeys start with a single step.

Once you have identified a specific dream, develop a plan. As an outline, you might want to list the goal, and then the steps to get you there. For example, imagine that you always wanted to take watercolor lessons. That is the goal. The steps to get there might include locating classes in your area, determining the cost, getting a list of materials, and so forth. As you work through the steps, your dream will move closer to reality.

In Appendixes C and D we have provided some journal suggestions, starter questions, a goals planner, and some space for you to begin your journey.

Carl Jung believed that the task of the second half of life is a solo quest to discover who we are in our deepest self, the self that exists apart from longtime roles. He emphasized enjoying the process more than focusing on results. The task of the second half of our lives, then, is to find our missing selves, to become whole.

You are entering the Wisdom Years, a creative lifetime juncture. "Another I is beginning." A wonderful journey lies ahead!

Chapter Sixteen
Disconnecting and Reconnecting

*Only through our connectedness to others
can we really know and enhance the self.
And only through working on the self can we
begin to enhance our connectedness to others.*

—Harriet Goldhor Lerner

 It is ironic that in disconnecting from our children when they become adults, we also reconnect with them. At this crossroads from child to adult, we need to consider them fully emancipated from us, and we from them. Our task is to disconnect as parents and reconnect as friends. The charge is to deal with each other as free individuals tied together by love and loyalty, not power, obligation or guilt. Just as our parents shed ideas and culture from fifty or sixty years ago, and we shed ideas and culture from thirty or forty years ago, our children will cut their cloth from twenty-first century material. Each family member needs to recognize that we are products of our own generational time and therefore need to resist forcing a set of beliefs, expectations or codes of behavior upon each other.

We can begin this next part of our lives simply by accepting the truth of what is. Our child has married and begun the most exciting, most committed adventure of his or her life. To think that this will not bring about changes is to deny reality.

> Roslyn thought she was prepared when her son married. She was actually happy that he had found someone to share his life. What she was not prepared for was how little she now sees of her son. Roslyn said she can never have a private talk with him without him repeating everything to his wife. Roslyn feels excluded from his life and she misses his company.

What Roslyn and others need to understand is that there has been a sea change in the relationship, and it is a permanent change. Roslyn has a sense of loss; however, this does not mean the love is gone. Elisabeth Kübler-Ross, in her seminal work about loss, lists the five stages of coping with loss: denial, anger, bargaining (*if only this isn't true, I'll be good...I'll pray every day...etc.*), depression, and, finally, acceptance (Kübler-Ross, 1969). When Roslyn accepts her reality, a new relationship will be forged out of the love they have for one another. Metamorphosing outworn parental roles does not mean mothering and fathering need to be less loving, less caring than before. It does mean these relationships will be based more on mutual respect and friendship than on biological ties, dependency needs and/or old habits. The sooner the acceptance of reality begins, the sooner the new relationship can be forged.

Elinor Lenz in *Once My Child...Now My Friend* advances the concept of the "ex-mother." She writes, "Once the adult child has reached maturity and left home to pursue a self-directing life, all links of dependency between parent and child are dissolved. No question, leaving home is a critical rite of passage for the parent as well as the child but once that is done, the remaining ties are friendship, understanding and acceptance of each other's individuality and independent life" (Lenz, 1981).

In other words, the parental license has expired and is not renewable. It is no longer advisable to tell our "children" what to do, how to think or how to behave. Those days are gone, and really, good riddance. Once you realize that you no longer need to parent in the same way, that you can put your energy into other aspects of your life, be it a partner, a hobby, grandchildren or what have you, you will begin to feel a huge weight of responsibility lifted from your shoulders. The relationship you will shape now with your child is adult to adult with all of those implications and pleasures. Disagreements and conflicts can be approached as negotiable, problem-solving situations. You no longer have to, nor should you, shield your children from pain, offer unsolicited advice, manipulate the course of events in their lives and/or play the guilt card. This is a tall order, and from time to time we may slip, but the more we can continue on this path, the happier and healthier we will all be.

New connections will be shaped. You will move closer, and affection will flow naturally without being forced. Remember, the objective of this transition is to achieve a relationship between equals coming together in love and friendship, sharing a common set of memories.

Ruth, a retired nurse, sees her transition this way:

"I like being a mother-in-law but I don't look at this in-law stage of life as something to please me anyway. The Bible tells us that a man should leave his mother and father and cleave only to his wife, so with my being older and supposedly wiser in experience, anyway, it seems to me it's up to the mom to figure out how to stay friends with her married kids and whoever they have chosen to share their lives with."

Ruth concludes by saying, "Well, that's my take on it. It has been fun putting it into words." We are glad she did.

Chapter Seventeen
Healing In-Law Rifts

What you need to know about the past is that no matter what has happened, it has all worked together to bring you to this very moment. And this very moment you can choose to make everything new. Right now.

—Wayne Dyer

 In-laws can bring such joy and such heartache, and the road to a harmonious relationship can be fraught with misunderstandings. To begin with, one of the principle ways to deal with an in-law relationship is to recognize and honor differences. It is sometimes a very daunting proposition to understand in-laws. However, a very necessary and thoughtful analysis can help you recognize your differences in worldview and temperaments, especially if differing opinions are present (or looming) in in-law conflicts. If no consensus can be reached, at least a recognition of these in-law differences allows the individuals to tactfully agree to disagree. Sometimes there are fundamental differences which are best left on the back burner. Perhaps at some future time, these differences will be easier to deal with. However, we do need to accept that some differences may never be resolved.

It is important to recognize that family relationships run hot and cold, and rarely remain fixed over a lifetime. Be patient. Reassessment may be an ongoing process and feelings for each other may go up and down. Problems that develop are like weeds, less than attractive but not likely to kill anyone. Let things simmer down when you are upset with an in-law issue and weigh it carefully. Then decide if it is worth the consequences of putting it on the table. Perhaps it is, but choose your battles carefully. Maintain respect at all costs. Also, beware of being dragged into a controversy where you are asked to take sides. If you haven't already realized this, no good can come from mixing into a fracas. Far better to remain aloof, keeping your own counsel and waiting until the dust settles.

In-laws who are able to *really* listen to each other with understanding and tolerance may find they do not need to change each other. We cannot alter in-law relationships by trying to control them; instead, the focus needs to be on changing ourselves in relation to the new family additions.

When everyone gets along, it makes it easier for the spouse to be a good husband or wife. When your children marry, their spouse comes first. Family relationships won't succeed under any other conditions.

Boundaries are essential if you want to be involved with your family and enjoy happy relationships. It is not easy to establish fair and comfortable limits and this may take some trial and error. Look on it as preventative maintenance. Setting guidelines in advance can head off a great deal of stress, misunderstanding and, yes, guilt and anger. Consider involving the other family members in setting up family expectations. In-laws are long-term relatives and learning to set limits with each other and thereby enjoying your relationship can be an important and rewarding part of your life.

Become a more skilled communicator...first, by getting more comfortable with using language to reveal rather than conceal—in other words, be honest and direct and, of course, diplomatic—and second, by listening attentively and hearing what is actually being said. Often people are so busy formulating a response that they really do not hear both the words and the underlying message before responding. Remember that *silent* and *listen* contain the same letters.

Be sensitive to your new role of in-law. Help out when you can but keep within your boundaries and wait to be invited to the home of your child and spouse. Learn about your new in-law's likes and dislikes. The average age for marriage in America is now twenty-five for women and twenty-seven for men so they have years of personal history to share with you. Get to know them and find out more about their childhoods and relationships with their relatives. Ask questions, listen to the answers, remember them. Accept daughters/sons-in-law as they are. They are as multidimensional as you are. This builds a solid foundation and will be very useful not only when the inevitable "tsunamis" hit but will generally enrich family life.

The more mothers-in-law and daughters-in-law speak, by phone or e-mail (if they don't have other regular contact), the more positive the relationship. Regular contacts are important and can serve to connect families whose physical contact is limited by geographic distance or other extenuating factors. Bonding often occurs when the mother-in-law sees her daughter-in-law through some personal difficulty. Both mother-in-law and daughter/son-in-law should aim for respect: love may or may not come, but respect always needs to be there.

As positive relationships develop between mothers-in-law and their in-laws, it opens up the opportunity for each to work out emotional issues with the other that may be unfinished with their own parental relationships. A mother-in-law can function as a second, less controlling mother and the in-law(s) can give the mother-in-law a chance to be a mother in a new relationship. This relationship, when successful, also provides deeper emotional bonds between husband and wife, daughter/son and mother.

Undeniably, holidays are one of the primary causes of tension among in-laws. This is another arena in which the reality of change comes in with full force. Long-held family traditions may be blown apart, religious and cultural differences may become more visible...in short, there is a great deal of room for misunderstanding and hurt feelings. The media and other outside forces put heavy expectations on families to celebrate holidays "the right way," the old way, the traditional way, and so forth. All of this emphasis generates high expectations which are bound to crash one way or another. A holiday has been described by Laurie E. Rozakis in *The Complete Idiot's Guide to Dealing With In-Laws* as "a time when families get together to celebrate key events, rekindle relationships, refuel feelings of familial love, and settle a few old scores" (Rozakis, 1998).

Balancing holiday schedule commitments with married children is fraught with black holes of misunderstanding, hurt feelings, and emotional consequences. The stress goes both ways while, ironically, the intent of the celebration is to bring pleasure to families, develop closer ties, and enjoy the holiday experience. It is quite possible that whatever your decision about what family members you choose to spend your holidays with, you are going to upset someone. Recognize that you can't be all things to all people but make a clear attempt to make a fair and balanced decision about which holiday you'd like to host and where you'll travel to celebrate others. Then announce it and move on. Do this as far in advance as possible, allowing other family members to make their plans. And, of course, be flexible as well as sensitive to everyone's needs, including your own and those of your spouse, and work your schedule accordingly. Making this emotionally laden decision calmly and clearly goes a long way toward your own peace and tranquility.

Difficulties arise because families may have different expectations. As long as you communicate clearly what you want and what you can do, people will generally handle honesty better than disappointment. And remember to value off-peak time. Most families who agonize over holidays don't spend enough time together the rest of the year. Spreading visits out during the year can take pressure off the holiday season.

Sometimes it is appropriate as well as more convenient to spend holiday times with only part of the family one year—and with different family members the next year. Time can be equalized over a period of years. The Buddhists have a saying: "Everything is in a constant state of change." If your child needs to miss his first Thanksgiving with you in twenty years, so be it. Close up the kitchen and take a cruise or go feed the hungry at the local mission.

When there are in-law estrangements, it takes time, energy, and forgiveness to end them. Sometimes this is very difficult. However, keeping the peace and letting go of anger and resentment will make you happier and healthier.

We offer these suggestions for more harmonious relations:

1. Keep the door open. Send birthday cards, notes, and e-mails just so your in-law will know you're always receptive; whenever they're ready to reenter your life, you'll be there.

2. Focus on what you can do to improve the situation rather than lay blame or worry about things you can't control.

3. Take preventative measures to head off an estrangement. If you believe an in-law is avoiding you, do something before it gets worse: the longer the time

lapse, the harder it is to mend. Be
flexible and call. Say, "You're important
to me and if I have done something
wrong, tell me. I want to make it right."

4.   Write a letter, saying something like "I'd
      like to make a fresh start" or "You're my
      family and I miss you." Be honest and
      loving, without accusations. Be very
      careful to keep your letter positive so it
      is not open to misinterpretation. Putting
      it in writing allows the recipient to think
      about what's been said without having
      to react immediately.

5.   Make a genuine apology if you are in
      the wrong. Apologizing is such a
      cleansing experience. It truly is a way to
      break down barriers and start fresh.

6.   If the estrangement is extended, suggest
      a low-key way to connect. Rather than
      get together to talk, which creates undue
      stress, do something where you can
      simply enjoy each other's company. Of
      course, this will depend on personal
      preferences. Some people love to shop,
      others hate the process. Some people
      love movies, museums, hiking or
      hanging out at the beach. Suggest
      whatever you think would serve the
      purpose, which is to reconnect in a non-

threatening atmosphere; just start the ball rolling. It is not important to replay old scenes such as *you said, I said*. Sometimes it is better to ease back into a relationship, forget past hurts, and just move on. You decide where you want the relationship to go.

7. Last, and perhaps most important, always assume good will. Remember the high hopes that surrounded the engagement and the wedding. The excitement, the joy, the pride. What happens afterwards when reality sets in and the stardust settles can change the dynamics. Still, if you can remember and recapture the feelings that were there at the beginning when everyone was happy and full of hope, and hold those feelings when you interact with your in-law, you will have succeeded in taking the high road. There is no better feeling.

Chapter Eighteen
Lessons Learned

We cannot change our past.
We cannot change the fact that people act
in a certain way. We cannot change the
inevitable. The only thing we can do is play on
the one string we have, and that is our attitude.
                                    —Charles R. Swindoll

Our goal from the beginning of this book has been to provide strategies and encouragement to women on their mother-in-law journey. We do this by describing the qualities of positive in-law relationships and by sharing the experience and wisdom of the many women who generously participated in our research for this book. We have included the struggles of in-law relationships that are troubled because they teach us, too.

Relationships with mothers-in-law often improve with age. A national poll of 1,000 people reveals that older people get along better with their mothers-in-law than younger people. People in their 40s, 50s and 60s are more likely to get along equally well with their own mothers and in-laws, while those in their 20s and 30s usually prefer their own mothers. As people mature, maybe some of the earlier gnarly issues mellow and take on a different perspective. It is amazing how the gift of time can change our outlook.

Dr. Terri Apter, of the University of Cambridge, offers her thoughts on how to encourage positive in-law relationships:

1. Responsiveness to a son- or daughter-in-law's needs and feelings;

2. Patience in face of a son- or daughter-in-law's coolness or suspicion; and

3. Sense of humor at family dynamics.

Our survey respondents came up with their own mother-in-law advice list.

1. *Pay attention to your in-law children. Help them only when needed.*

Barbara tells us, "Our first grandchild was born profoundly deaf and it was difficult to know what to do and how to help since no one in the family had any experience with deaf culture and its impact on the family. We took the position the parents were intelligent and well-educated, and when or if we were needed we'd be asked. It worked out fine. Be there and helpful when needed but be quiet until then!"

Tina comments that it is challenging trying to accept that her son is a man and no longer needs her help. She concludes, "He just needs my love and support."

Laurie suggests, "I think there's a mutual sense of appreciation when we help each other in times of need: babysitting, moving, caring for new mothers in the family. I try to do small things, also, like fixing their favorite foods during visits."

Beth recommends, "Sometimes make it a point to call and talk to the in-law kid. It builds a relationship foundation."

Rita thinks, "It is important, if your son- or daughter-in-law is a good, decent person, to love them unconditionally if they make your child happy. Your child's happiness in the marriage is the most important thing. Hopefully, love on your terms will come later."

Louise is very attentive to the relationship she is building with her son-in-law and works at being friendly, not just his wife's mother.

Sherrie tells us her mother-in-law came to help her when she was ill. "She could put a potato and an onion together and make the whole house smell good and make you feel there was something else going on in there besides sickness."

Sally says, "Long before my children were married, I made up my mind that if someone loved my child, I would love them. I still feel very strongly about this."

2. *Be pleasant, non-demanding.*

Dana doesn't want to be a pain like her mother-in-law was and wanted to make sure issues worked out harmoniously among all her family members. "When there are problems, differences are talked over and resolved to everyone's satisfaction."

Diana feels, "If you don't like your son- or daughter-in-law, you have to learn to like and accept them and give them the benefit of the doubt if you can."

Lillian believes in "Accepting that the life my married children live is different from mine, and I can enjoy the difference."

3.   *Be a living example of the behavior you would like in return.*

Darcy stresses we all must respect each other and treat each other as we would like to be treated. "I take great pride in the fact my children ask me to visit them and actually enjoy my company and seek my advice on occasion. I can't stress too much, we all respect each other and treat each other as we would like to be treated."

Kay says, "I treat everyone the way I would like to be treated…with consideration and kindness. I do not mix into my adult children's affairs, and listen carefully when they ask for my viewpoint. I try to be objective and understanding."

4.   *Keep everyone included.*

Some families have entrenched habits of communication which exclude and include depending on who the communicator is and the state of their relationships. This is a very divisive practice fraught with misunderstandings and worse. Every effort needs to be made to include all the family in the loop where important family information is concerned.

5. *Be aware of the power of words and how they may be perceived.*

    Monica says she does not say anything when she feels critical of her daughter-in-law. "I try to give sympathy when something goes wrong, praise when something is modestly positive and not volunteer my opinion or solution. I have a self-centered daughter-in-law. I would love to be closer to her but think her insecurities do not allow her to be open with me. We get along best when we talk about how bright/clever/wonderful her daughter is."

6. *Base your relationship on spiritual principles and mutual family values.*

    Carey has found that letting go and letting God take care of her children is best for her. "To be a part of their lives but not in the role of mother…but rather as a spectator and a family member. This is difficult at times but I love them enough to work hard on letting go and letting God take care of them."

    Dee shares, "Our heritage of Christian faith was primary to our family lives. We all worshipped together and saw my parents and grandparents live their faith on a daily basis. My husband and I have managed to pass on this heritage to our sons and I see this same dynamic continuing. Our daughters-in-law come from stable, healthy families. For some reason this seems to perpetuate itself and I believe affects in-law relationships in a positive way."

7. *Work on staying in close communication and involved with the family.*

Anita works on finding common ground on which to build a relationship with her daughter-in-law. "Even though she is not the type of person I would seek out as a companion, I go to great lengths to find ways to connect and be a friend of hers."

8. *Be accepting.*

Robin tells us, "I am smart enough to know the shortcomings of my children and because of that I find I can more easily see both sides...not just my child's side."

Juanita shares that it was challenging but very important to accept a "stranger" into her family with "all his quirks, likes and dislikes, habits and prejudices that were so different from ours."

Rebecca observes, "All families are different. Our own family's ideals and values may not always coincide with those of our son-in-law. I accept that."

9. *Give an opinion only when asked.*

    When her married children and their spouses ask for advice, Marie says, "I reason with them and help them see both sides of the picture. They ask why I have to be so open-minded and make them see things from different perspectives. But it usually works out and the problem gets fixed."

    Amy notes that her adult children sometimes want and ask her opinion and other times may ask but they don't WANT it!!! "Trying to figure out the difference and keeping my mouth closed is a challenge."

    Tina tries to avoid commenting on a few child-rearing issues that bother her. She concludes that over time these issues may be outgrown so, in the long run, it is more important to maintain a good relationship than to have things done her way. "Thinking before I say something, though, is sometimes difficult, but fortunately our daughter-in-law is both forgiving and endowed with a sense of humor."

Dolly states, "Remembering I am not the mother in charge of all things has been helpful for me. I cannot control or direct behaviors, habits, or child rearing in my children's homes. I must bite my tongue sometimes and be supportive of new ways. When asked for my opinion I must be honest and diplomatic as well as sensitive to how it is received."

Heide's practice is to listen carefully to her children. "We may not always agree on how we'd do this or that but usually, if left alone, we all end up in the same place anyway."

Amber believes in, "Not automatically taking my son's side, not leaping in to protect him and to let him and his wife establish THEIR relationship on THEIR terms."

De Weese offers, "Don't butt in. Offer advice only when asked. Of course, if absolutely necessary, Machiavellian approach may be advisable if tongue hurts too much." While we appreciate the humor expressed here, we don't advocate the Machiavellian practice.

10. *Never show up unannounced, uninvited.*

Catherine suggests, "Calling a day or at least several hours before your arrival time would be appreciated; think how you feel when people drop in unexpectedly."

11. *Be positive. Each generation has different expectations.*

Ramona feels, "Each adult family member is responsible for their own home and has learned different ways of doing things. Certain things may be more important to one generation than the next. Certain niceties that one family may observe may not be familiar or comfortable for the other generation."

12. *Accept people as they are. Be considerate and generous.*

Lydia recommends, "Respect for individual personalities and strengths brings admiration instead of dwelling on negatives. There is much to be gained and nothing really to lose by staying open and positive. If all else fails and you run into a 'wall,' walk around it. Wait. And try again."

13. *Remember your sense of humor.*

Carol comments, "Being an in-law is a difficult relationship. When I married my husband, my mother-in-law was very unhappy and never liked me until senility set in and now I am her best friend. It just goes to show you that if you wait long enough, life will change."

We definitely see these advice lists as two-way streets. Each family member has equal responsibility to make the relationships harmonious and happy. Mothers-in-law should not be expected to bear more than their fair share.

Remember, the only person we have control over is ourselves. While sometimes we may be very frustrated with our in-law situation and lose control of our feelings, we can choose what to do with these feelings and how we will respond to challenges before us. When we raised our children, we told them being angry did not hurt the object of their anger; it only hurt the one who was angry. We need to follow our own advice.

What is, is. When your child marries a person who is difficult for you to accept, it often feels like a loss that must be grieved. But what you feel today may change tomorrow. As the Serenity Prayer reminds us: "God, grant me the serenity to accept the things I cannot change, the courage to change the things I can, and the wisdom to know the difference."

Whenever possible, start with the premise that everyone wants less strife and conflict in their family relationships…and their lives. People may start out with good intentions and then somehow get off track. Remember this even when you're angry and hurt. Make an effort to look at the situation from the in-law's point of view.

We are responsible for our own happiness. We choose to do what we want to do with our time, money, and life. It is not selfish to make choices that please us. You may choose to spend time with friends, volunteer, go back to work, babysit grandchildren, work out, take up cake decorating or figure drawing, or go on a solo vacation. The list of possibilities is endless. The bottom line is understanding that making healthy choices, so long as it doesn't interfere with the rights of others, puts us on the road to true fulfillment.

Bear in mind that it's never over no matter what the situation. There is *always* a chance that things will get better. In time, they often do. And as you grow and evolve, richer family relationships also evolve. Life is full of surprises. Once in a while there is a shift in the mobile and balance is once more achieved.

The women whose stories are the basis of this book have shown us that opening to the new relationships which come from acquiring in-laws can be "like rain falling on the hard-packed soil of our lives. If we are willing, it can soften us so we can feel gratitude and compassion and our own human vulnerability."[1]

Let it rain.

[1] Anderson & Hopkins, *The Feminine Face of God.*

Appendixes

Appendix A.

Mother-in-Law Bill of Rights and Responsibilities

RIGHTS	RESPONSIBILITIES
You have the right to be treated with respect and courtesy.	You have the responsibility to treat everyone with respect and courtesy.
You have the right to privacy.	You have the responsibility to afford others privacy.
You have the right to freedom of opinion and expression voiced carefully and with love.	You have the responsibility to allow others freedom of opinion and expression with the same care and love.
You have the right to live your own life in the way you choose.	You have the responsibility to allow others to live their own lives the way they choose.
You have the right to be treated fairly and openly.	You have the responsibility to treat others fairly and openly.
You have the right to your feelings.	You have the responsibility to acknowledge the feelings of others.

Appendix B.
"I" Messages

"I" messages are a way to positively communicate your feelings without putting your partner on the defensive. "I" messages help to ease strain in conversations, and encourage honest communication. "I" messages rather than "you" messages automatically defuse tension, encourage open, honest communication and help to define and articulate the problem.

It is useful to use "I" messages when there are stressful or challenging situations, and when it is important to get your point of view across without being insulting or demeaning or putting the other person on the defensive.

There are three basic components to an "I" message:

1. Identify the problem behavior, i.e., what's irritating you.

2.   Share how this irritating behavior makes you feel.

3.   Explain the consequences of your feelings.

A typical sentence structure for an "I" message goes something like this.

I feel_____(state what you are feeling)

when you_____(describe the activity)

because_____(link the action to your feeling).

Rather than,

"You never call me anymore," work on this:

"I feel sad when you don't call because I miss your company."

Rather than,

"You never want to spend time with me alone," work on this:

"I feel hurt when you go into another room when I come over, because I want time alone with you so that we can connect with each other."

Rather than,

"You never let me feed the children at my house," work on this:

"I feel so rejected when you tell the children not to eat at my house because the message I get is that my food is not good enough for the children and that I would somehow willfully harm them."

"I" messages can also be used to encourage people.

"I like the colors you chose for the couch."

"I'm so happy that you chose to tell me that."

Pay attention to what others say to you. Practice changing "you" statements into "I" messages. At first it may sound a little stilted, but with practice, it will become a natural way of speaking.

Appendix C.

Journal / Notes

 There is no right or wrong way to begin a journal. You simply begin. Some people choose to begin by writing about the physical aspects of their room, the weather, and/or how they are physically feeling. Once the process begins, it will take you naturally to deeper thoughts and emotions. Remember, no one will ever see this journal without your permission.

Sometimes a sentence completion exercise can help you get started. For example:

Today was a good (bad) day because…

Today I learned…

My husband (partner, child, boss)…

I wish…

I am happiest when…

I love to…

I hate to…

I was frightened when…

Appendix D.
Lists / Goals

Ten things I would like to do with my life:

1.
2.
3.
4.
5.
6.
7.
8.
9.
10.

Now prioritize those items.

Now take the first item and begin a set of objectives to reach that goal.

Remember, the journey of a thousand miles begins with a single step.

Bibliography

Anderson, S. R., & Hopkins, P. (1991). *The feminine face of god: The unfolding of the sacred in women.* New York: Bantam Books.

Angier, N. (1999). *Woman: An intimate biography.* New York: Houghton Mifflin Company.

Apter, T. (2007, August 31). *Mother-in-law stories* (Internet advice page).

Averick, L. (1996). *Don't call me mom: How to improve your in-law relationships.* Florida: Lifetime Books, Inc.

Barash, S. S. (2001). *Mothers-in-law and daughters-in-law, love, hate, rivalry and reconciliation.* Far Hills, NJ: New Horizon Press.

Bradshaw, J. (1988). *Bradshaw on: The family.* Deerfield Beach, FL: Health Communications, Inc.

Brenner, P. H. (2000). *Seeing your life through new eyes.* Hillsborough, OR: Beyond Words Publishing.

Carlson, R. (1997). *You can be happy no matter what,* p. 39. Novato, CA: New World Library.

Cotterill, P. (1992). But for freedom, you see, not to be a babyminder: Women's attitudes towards grandmother care. *Sociology, 26*(4), 603(16).

———. (1995). *Friendly relations? mothers and daughters-in-law.* London: Taylor and Francis.

Dinnerstein, D. (1977). *The mermaid and the minotaur.* New York: Harper & Row.

Duvall, E. (1954). *In-laws pro and con.* New York: Associated Press.

EPIC/MCR poll. (1996, May 27). Relationships with mothers-in-law improve with age, poll shows. *Jet, 90*(2), 12(1).

Erikson, E. (1959). *Identity and the life cycle.* New York: W.W. Norton & Company, Inc.

Felder, L. (2003). *When difficult relatives happen to good people.* Emmans, PA: Rodale.

Fields, R. (2001, August 20). Unwed partners up 72% in the U.S. *Los Angeles Times,* pp. 1, 13.

Goode, S. (2000, June 5). Mothers-in-law truly are loved. *Insight on the News, 16*(121), 4.

Greider, L. (2000, March/April). How not to be a monster-in-law. *Modern Maturity,* 57-81.

Gullette, M. M. (2000, April 2). Why America has to judge Amy's mother. *The New York Times,* p. 34.

Hargrave, T. (2001, November/December). Holiday burnout. *Modern Maturity,* 32-34.

Harvard Women's Health Watch. (2000, September 1). Women, work and stress. *Harvard Women's Health Watch, VIII*(1).

Horsley, G. (1996). *In-laws: A guide to extended family therapy.* New York: John Wiley & Sons.

———. (1997). *The in-law survival guide: How to prevent—and solve—in-law problems.* New York: John Wiley & Sons.

———. (1997, Spring). In-laws: Extended family therapy. *The American Journal of Family Therapy, 25*(Spring), 18-27.

Jackson, J., & Berg-Cross, L. (1988, July 1). Extending the extended family: The mother-in-law and daughter-in-law relationship of black women. *Family Relations, 37*(3), 293-97.

Jarvis, C. (2001). *The marriage sabbatical, the journey that brings you home.* New York: Perseus Publishing.

Kubler-Ross, E. (1969). *On death and dying.* New York: Macmillan Publishing Co.

Lamb, B. (1997). *Booknotes: America's finest authors on reading, writing, and the power of ideas.* New York: Times Books.

Lenz, E. (1981). *Once my child...now my friend.* New York: Warner Books.

Lippman, W. (1922). *Public opinion.*

Marks, J. (1987, April 1). We have a problem. *Parents' Magazine,* 82-85.

Marotz-Baden, R. & Mattheis, C. Daughters-in-law and stress in two generation farm families. (1994). *Family Relations, 43,* 132-137.

Michael, R. T. (In editing). An economic perspective on sex, marriage and the family in contemporary United States. In S. Tipton & J. J. Witte (Eds.), *The modern family in interdisciplinary perspective.* Berkeley: University of California Press.

Mutunhc, S. (2000, August 29). Beat empty-nester blues. *The Desert Sun,* sec. D, pp. 1,6.

Nolen-Hoeksema, S. (2003). *Women who think too much.* New York: Henry Holt.

O'Connor, E. (2001, April 1). Can't get no satisfaction. *Monitor on Psychology, American Psychological Association, 32*(4), 13.

People. (2000, August 21). Mamma mia! *People,* 85.

Pipher, M. (1999). *Another country: Navigating the emotional terrain of our elders.* New York: Riverhead Books.

Raddatz, M. (1995, April 1). How to handle mother-in-law power plays. Family Life: Relationships. *Parents Magazine, 70*(4), 97.

Rozakis, L. (1998). *The complete idiot's guide: Dealing with in-laws.* New York: Alpha Books.

Sheehy, G. (1995). *New passages: Mapping your life across time.* New York: Ballantine Books.

Strom, S. (2001, April 22). On the rise in Japan: Assertive daughters-in-law. *The New York Times International (New York),* p. 3.

Taitz, S. (1990, April 8). Love with a proper stranger. *The New York Times Magazine, 139,* 14.

Tannen, D. (2001). *I only say this because I love you, how the way we talk can make or break family relationships throughout our lives.* New York: Random House.

Terry, T. M. (2001). *In-laws and marital relationships.* Unpublished. A master of science thesis, California State University, San Bernardino.

Viahoutsikou, C. (1997). Mothers-in-law and daughters-in-law: Politicizing confrontations. *Journal of Modern Greek Studies, 15*(2), 283-302.

Viorst, J. (1986). *Necessary losses: The loves, illusions, dependencies and impossible expectations that all of us have to give up in order to grow.* New York: Simon and Schuster.

Wallerstein, J., & Blakeslee, B. (1995). *The good marriage.* New York: Warner Books.

Watson, B. (2000). The amazing author of Oz. *Smithsonian, (31)*3, 112-120.

Wegscheider, S. (1981). *Another chance.* Palo Alto, CA: Science and Behavior Books, Inc.

Womble, D. L. (1966). *Foundations for marriage and family relations.* New York: Macmillan.

CPSIA information can be obtained
at www.ICGtesting.com
Printed in the USA
LVOW10s1428280518
578743LV00001B/32/P